Nature Reflections

Outdoor Devotional Series

Nature Reflections

Patty Mondore

North Wind Publishing

Brewer, Maine

North Wind Publishing
P.O. Box 3655
Brewer, ME 04412
northwindpublishing.com

10 9 8 7 6 5 4 3 2 1

ISBN 978-0-9895689-0-6

Library of Congress Control Number: 2013942607

All photos by the author unless otherwise indicated.

Bookstores/Giftshops: Bulk ordering is available. Contact info@northwindpublishing.com. Also available through Ingram and Spring Arbor Distributors.

Dedication

As we put the finishing touches on this second book in my
Outdoor Devotional Series, *I find my heart welling up with*
thanksgiving, once again, for the husband God has given me
to share life and his creation with. I love you, Bob. I am also
thankful to you, dear reader, for joining me on my nature
adventures. And above all, I am so thankful to the Lord for this
beautiful world and, even more, for the one yet to come.

Publisher's Note

In the beginning, God created . . . (Gen. 1:1)

Nature Reflections by Patty Mondore is one book in a series of devotionals for people who love the outdoors. *Nature Reflections* is the second book in the series. As a person who loves the outdoors, I could relate to each story in some way, having had similar experiences while I was enjoying nature. Experiencing a beautiful vista overlooking water, gazing up at mountains or looking closely at the details of a flower or insect brings one closer to God as we admire His handiwork.

Nature Reflections is a 90-day Devotional and Journal to help you with your bible study and meditations. Each day starts with a beautiful black and white nature photo and bible verse. *The Trek,* steers you toward portions of the bible you should read that day while *Nature Reflections* are the author's personal experiences enjoying nature and where she relates that experience to biblical teachings. *Nature's Journal* is an area for the reader to write down personal thoughts for the day, so this book becomes a keepsake journal. May God bless you and yours.

JANET ROBBINS, Publisher

Devotions in Nature

There is something built into the human heart that responds to the beauty of the natural world we live in. Whether it is a spectacular blazing sunset, the tranquility of a lake on a still day, the scents and colors of a garden, or the melodious voices of the songbirds, when we take the time to stop and really take it in—to experience it—we are moved. I can't help but to think that being made in the image of God means, in part, that we were created with the ability to appreciate the works of his hands as no other one of his creatures can. When we find ourselves captivated by creation and also acknowledge the one who formed it, our experience often turns to worship. At that point, our response is not only natural, but has become supernatural.

Nature Reflections is a 90-day devotional that will take you on a trek through God's created world and his written Word. Beginning in Genesis and ending in Revelation, each reading starts with a Scripture verse and a passage to read, followed by some thoughts that will point out how nature has illustrated these verses to us. The chapters include nature facts and scientific tidbits about the world we live in, and how those facts are evidences that point to its Creator. There will also be plenty of lighthearted stories about the many creatures and true wildlife encounters I have had. And most important, wherever the trail takes us, it will ultimately end up leading us back to the loving hands of the Master Designer, himself.

So, I invite you to come join me on this 90-day trek outdoors. As I share a few of the natural wonders of this amazing world, I hope that you will find your heart lifted up in supernatural praise to the one who made it all, and who did so with us in mind.

PATTY MONDORE

Nature Reflections

1. In the Beginning

In the beginning, God created the heavens and the earth.
(Gen. 1:1)

The Trek:

Read Gen 1:1-2 and Psalm 33:1-11

Nature Reflections:

In the Beginning, or at least in the beginning of our chapter in eternity, God's first act was to create the natural world we live in. In preparation for our arrival, he designed a spectacular universe with a planet perfectly suited for not just life, but human life. When his masterpiece was complete he invited us to its unveiling. Well, almost complete. Actually, his guests of honor were the finishing touch on his masterpiece. God created the sun and stars, the earth, its oceans, mountains, flora and fauna and said, "It is good." But his work was not quite finished. The Lord of the Universe then decided to create someone who could appreciate all he had done. He custom-designed his last creation to see his universe with the same kind of eyes as the Master Artist himself. He made us, and only us, in his image with the ability to see, hear, sense, and experience the wonders built into every detail of his creation.

1

It is no wonder, then, that we are inspired by nature. God wanted to share his artwork with us and made us with a capacity to appreciate it as no other creature could. So when you find your heart racing at the sight of a glorious sunset, or at the cry of a loon, don't worry—it's only natural. However, God had much more in mind for us than just to be his art critics. We were created to enjoy his creation but, even more, to know, love and be loved by the Artist, himself. One of the ways God has chosen to reveal himself to us is through his Creation. So, when you see that sunset and find your heart welling up with praise for its Maker, don't worry—rejoice! It's only natural!

Nature Journal

2. Light

> *And God said, "Let there be light,"*
> *and there was light.*
> *(Gen. 1:3)*

The Trek:

Read Gen. 1:3-8 and John 1:1-9

Nature Reflections:

The alarm went off and before I even opened my eyes I felt
the pressures of the day ahead. It was the busiest time of year
at work and I felt overwhelmed by the demands awaiting
me there. I got up and looked out the window hoping for
some inspiration. All I saw was an overcast sky blanketing
the world in a predawn gray. The drab scene only added to
the oppressiveness I was attempting to shake. I pulled out
my Bible, thankful that I wasn't dependent on the weather
for inspiration. As the Psalmist put it, ". . . where does my
help come from? My help comes from the LORD, the Maker
of heaven and earth" (Ps. 121:1,2). I felt the pressures being
lifted off of my shoulders as I read. I closed the Bible and
looked up just as the room became flooded with light. The
clouds had parted and the sun was clearing the horizon with
the blaze of a rocket launch. The waters on the lake below

shimmered in its light. Quite suddenly the world had transformed from darkness to light. By that time, so had I.

In one of his earliest recorded acts, God created light. It was the first step he took in turning chaos into order. When Jesus came to earth he, too, came to turn chaos from order—not in the physical world, but in the spiritual darkness of a fallen humankind. Jesus was "The true light that gives light to every man" (Jn. 1:9). Without him our lives were "without form and void." He came to be a Light in our lives that even bad weather and difficult days cannot dampen. I don't remember now whether the sun stayed out, but the Son continued to shine in my heart throughout that entire day.

Nature Journal

3. Garden of the Great Spirit

And God said, "Let the water under the sky be gathered to one place, and let dry ground appear." And it was so. God called the dry ground "land," and the gathered waters he called "seas." And God saw that it was good. (Gen. 1:9, 10)

The Trek:
Read Gen 1:9-19 & Ps 104:1-13

Nature Reflections:
I have to admit that whenever I read the portion of the Creation Account written above, I am always tempted to make my own minor adjustment to it. I can't help thinking that it should read, "and the gathered waters he called 'The Thousand Islands.' " The St. Lawrence Seaway is the longest inland waterway in the world. It forms a 2,340 mile natural border between Canada and the United States from the Atlantic Ocean to Lake Superior, in Minnesota. A 35-mile stretch of it is referred to as the Thousand Islands because it literally contains over 1800 islands. The area is so lovely the Native Americans in the area called it "man-I-to-anna" which means, "Garden of the Great Spirit." I couldn't agree more.

Geologists tell us that the Thousand Islands were originally part of a mountain range that was as majestic as the Rockies. The area lies on a ridge composed primarily of granite that joins the Canadian Shield with the Adirondack Mountains in New York. Over time, glaciers and rivers reduced the peaks to what are now the islands and shoals. In geological terms, the region is a "flooded landscape." I think I prefer the Garden of the Great Spirit, myself.

All of that geology may indeed be the scientific explanation of how he did it. Being a musician (and not a geologist) I can only take their word for it. What I do know is that once he finished separating the land from the waters, bringing order to chaos, and planting his Thousand Islands Garden, our Creator God looked at it, along with the rest of the marvelous world he made and said, "It is good." I couldn't agree more unless, of course, I was to make my own minor adjustment and call it "very good!"

Nature Journal

4. Colors

Photo by Simon Pierre Barrett

And God said, "Let the water teem with living creatures, and let birds fly above the earth across the expanse of the sky." So God created . . . every winged bird according to its kind. And God saw that it was good.
(Gen. 1:20, 21)

The Trek:
Read Genesis 1:20-31

Nature Reflections:
I love springtime! It is that glorious time of year when the earth begins to awaken from its winter slumber. The world slowly changes from gray and dead to being filled with the colors of new life. Spring also marks the return of some of its wildlife. The migratory birds reappear filling the air with their melodious voices. Other birds, those hardier species that remain throughout the year, celebrate the return of spring by changing colors. In particular, we love to watch the finches exchange their drab winter apparel for their glorious spring finery. The goldfinches turn from a grayish brown to a strikingly bright yellow, while the house finches go from dull brown to brilliant red. However, it is only the males of both species who make this dramatic seasonal transformation while

their female counterparts for the most part remain the same. Finches are among many bird species where the male is covered with vividly colorful plumage while the female's colors are very plain. Species such as cardinals, pheasants, and mallard ducks share this male/female contrast.

In addition to the sheer beauty of these male birds, God had a practical purpose in mind when he designed them with such dramatic spring colors. Springtime is breeding season and the bright colored plumage helps the male birds attract mates. Studies have actually demonstrated that brightly colored male finches are more successful at attracting mates than duller males. So, while we are enjoying the lovely spring fashion show taking place among our feathered friends, they are doing exactly what they were designed to do to survive and, in fact, flourish. God formed them with just what they needed to procreate and he did it with an artistic flair. No wonder when he finished creating the birds he exclaimed, "It is good!"

Nature Journal

5. Caretakers

*The LORD God took the man and put him in the
Garden of Eden to work it and take care of it.*
(Gen. 2:15)

The Trek:
Read Genesis 2:1-25

Nature Reflections:

As I sat on the dock enjoying the picture perfect day, the
tranquil scene was suddenly marred by a beer can floating
down the River. I grabbed a stick and attempted to snag it
as a part of my own personal Save-The-River campaign. As
I retrieved my prize I felt a sense of satisfaction. Small as it
was, I had done my part in keeping the River clean and the
wildlife safe from humankind's pollution and waste. Protecting the environment really is the Christian thing to do. After
all, it was God, himself, who gave us the original commission when he told Adam and Eve to care for the earth. Jesus
reinforced the importance of caring for the creatures of the
earth when he said, "If one of you has a son or an ox that
falls into a well on the Sabbath day, will you not immediately
pull him out?" (Lk. 14:5). He also revealed the Father's heart
for his creatures when he asked, "Are not five sparrows sold

for two pennies? Yet not one of them is forgotten by God . . . Consider how the lilies grow . . . not even Solomon in all his splendor was dressed like one of these" (Lk. 6:12:6,27).

Yet, as believers, some of us have not been faithful with the assignment we've been given to care for the earth. Many of us have dissociated ourselves from some of the environmental movements based on political, philosophical and even spiritual differences. Unfortunately, we have chosen to ignore the issue altogether. It is true that some of these "Save-the-Planet" groups have very different motivations than believers (to be discussed in another chapter). We who truly worship the Creator, however, should have an even greater appreciation of his creation and desire to bear the honor of being his caretakers.

Nature Journal

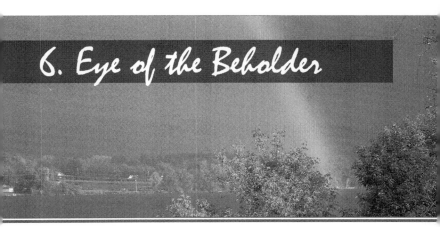

6. Eye of the Beholder

*I have set my rainbow in the clouds, and it will be the
sign of the covenant between me and the earth.*
(Gen. 9:13)

The Trek:
Read Genesis 9:1-17

Nature Reflections:
As I drove to prayer meeting, the storm began. Drenching
rain and crashing thunder engulfed my little car. As I listened to the prayers of the believers interspersed between
rolls of thunder, I felt as though we were storming the gates
of heaven. By the time we were done, so was the storm. The
giant arc of a magnificent rainbow greeted us as we exited
the church. The very first rainbow followed the worst storm
in earth's history. The rainbow was a symbol of God's promise to Noah and his decedents to never allow the waters to
completely destroy mankind again. The Bible tells us *why* we
see the rainbow, but we now better understand *how* we see
it. That beautiful band of color is really the sunlight spread
out into its spectrum of colors and diverted to the eye of the
observer by water droplets. The center of the rainbow's arc is
located on an imaginary line extending from the sun through

the observer's eye to the water drops. That means no two people actually see the same rainbow.

God's Word has something in common with the rainbow. It is the Light—the one and universal truth. Yet, it speaks to every individual in a unique and personal way. Unfortunately, some do not see the light at all. They try to read the Bible and it is meaningless to them. Seeing assumes sight, and spiritual sight requires the Holy Spirit. God freely gives his Spirit to all who ask. As John Newton put it, "I once was lost, but now am found; was blind, but now I see." Anyone who has seen the Light and has begun to discover the wonders found in his word would readily agree that beauty truly is in the eye of the beholder.

Nature Journal

7. Astronomy, B.C.

Look up at the heavens and count the stars
—if indeed you can count them.
(Gen. 15:5)

The Trek:

Read Gen 15:1-6 and Psalm 147:1-11

Nature Reflections:

I love looking into the night sky. I call it stargazing. Those who do it professionally call it astronomy. Astronomy is the science dealing with all the celestial bodies in the universe. Did you know there are over 1000 stars that can be observed by the naked eye? The first charts mapping those stars were completed in 129 B.C. by Greek astronomer Hipparchus who cataloged and charted approximately 1000 stars believing he had successfully mapped the entire universe. The invention of the telescope in the 1600s revealed that a thousand stars didn't even scratch the surface of what lies beyond the limits of our earthly vision. Suddenly, we discovered we were living in a universe filled with stars beyond our ability to count. We are one small planet in a galaxy made up of about a million million stars. The Milky Way is but one of many great galaxies that populate our universe, some of them as distant as several billion light-years away.

Now what's interesting about Astronomy, B.C., is that the authors of the Bible were millennia ahead of the scientists of their day. While Hipparchus was cataloging his 1000-star universe, Jeremiah was writing, "I will make the descendants of David . . . as countless as the stars of the sky" (Jer. 33:22). During the writing of the Bible the Nation of Israel grew to become hundreds of thousands of people. Today, there are millions. In fact, because the Jewish people are scattered all over the world they are, indeed, countless. So, the Bible not only gave us good prophecy but good science. But then, its Author is the one who created those stars in the first place. They may be countless to us but "He determines the number of stars and calls them each by name" (Ps. 147:4).

Nature Journal

8. Thou Shalt Not Steal

You shall not steal.
(Deut. 5:19)

The Trek:
Read Deut 5:1-22

Nature Reflections:

Someone stole all the bait! We had hung a bait bucket full of live minnows in the water by the dock. By morning, something or someone had broken into the bucket and had eaten every last fish! A few days later I got to meet our bait thief face to face. I was sitting down by water when I sensed I was being watched. I spun around in time to see a tiny head disappear into the rocks by the water. A few minutes later, as I stared nervously at the rocks the little brown head reappeared and a small creature peered up at me for several seconds before popping back down again. On its third appearance I recognized the fuzzy-faced creature as a mink. "So you're the culprit!" I exclaimed as he scampered down the rocks and disappeared. The cute little guy hardly looked like a common crook. Nevertheless, despite their charming appearance, minks are known to be very aggressive carnivores that will eat anything they can catch (or steal). They are members of the weasel family distinguished by their rich dark fur. They have a long body and, being amphibious creatures, have webbed feet perfect for swimming (and opening bait buckets).

My cute little mink visitor is not really to blame for his invasion of someone else's goods. His relentless pursuit of prey is driven by the instinct given to him by God. A mink does not live by the same moral code we humans do. As far as I know, there are no "Ten Commandments for Critters." No, God's law was given solely to us humans— not to put an impossible burden on us but to help us realize our need for a God of grace. It is the need he was just dying to fulfill.

Nature Journal

9. Ben Franklin's Eagle

Photo courtesy Yathin S Krishnappa

But the LORD said to Samuel, "Do not consider his appearance or his height, for I have rejected him. The LORD does not look at the things man looks at. Man looks at the outward appearance, but the LORD looks at the heart."
(1 Sam. 16:7)

The Trek:
Read 1 Samuel 16:1-13

Nature Reflections:

"Look out for the turkeys" I cautioned my husband, Bob, as we headed toward camp. Now I admit I'm not always referring to wildlife when I use that expression, but today there was a flock of turkeys standing at the side of the road. Wild turkeys are known to be opportunistic feeders, meaning they'll eat just about anything they can swallow. So the side of the road is as good a place as any for them to find goodies. Not what I would consider the loveliest of creatures, the males in particular (gobblers, as they are called), have all kinds of appendages other fowl do not. In addition to their beard, a bristly mass of feathers on the breast, the gobblers have a fleshy growth called a wattle that hangs underneath their chin. They also have growths called caruncles on the side and back of the neck. The fleshy flap that hangs over the bill is called a snood (no, I'm not making this up). Good looks aside, wild turkeys have very sharp eyesight, can fly up to 55 miles per hour, and run at over 12 miles per hour.

To some of us, any creature with that many odd body parts rightfully deserves the humorous connotations it gets. Others, however, see this creature through an entirely different set of eyes. Benjamin Franklin so admired the bird that he wanted to make it the United States national symbol. Thankfully, God does not judge us humans by the same standards I have judged the turkey. He looks at the heart. He is not concerned about skin color, physical attractiveness, financial status, IQ, or athletic ability. When he sees the heart of someone who has put their trust in him, he never sees a turkey. We are eagles in his eyes.

Nature Journal

10. Has Beans

Have you not put a hedge around him and his household and everything he has? You have blessed the work of his hands, so that his flocks and herds are spread throughout the land.
(Job 1:10)

The Trek:
Read Job 1:1-12 and Job 42:10-17

Nature Reflections:

Every year I look forward to my parents' fresh, homegrown green beans. Their garden generally produces enough beans to freeze and last us through most of the winter. One year things started out as usual with a crop of healthy bean plants shooting out of the ground. My mouth was already watering thinking about those green beans. On my next visit, however, my dad took me out to the garden and showed me nothing but level ground where the plants had been. It had been stripped clean by rabbits. Forget the beans, themselves. These voracious gluttons hadn't even left stalks. Suddenly, after having spent most of my life sympathizing with Peter Rabbit, I found myself in complete solidarity with Mr. McGregor. The poor man has obviously been misjudged all these years. Getting back to our own garden ordeal, the following year my dad was prepared for the bunnies. He put a chicken wire fence around the entire garden and we were able to enjoy green beans right through until the following spring.

In the spiritual realm, growing believers can be as vulnerable to attacks as our bean crop had been. We have a very real enemy who the Scriptures tell us is lurking around all the time just "looking for someone to devour" (1 Pet. 5:8). But have no fear, believer! As tender young plants growing in God's garden we have the absolute assurance of a protection far more impenetrable than chicken wire. God has placed his hedge of protection around each of us. The Holy Spirit protects us from within while he has assigned his angelic force to surround and protect us from without. If Satan were to mess with any of them, he is the one who would most certainly end up as a "Has Bean."

Nature Journal

11. Ask the Animals

But ask the animals, and they will teach you . . .
(Job 12:7a)

The Trek:
Read Job 12:1-13

Nature Reflections:
As if Job hadn't gone through enough! He lost his family, his possessions, and his health. If he thought he might find some solace in his friends, he was mistaken. Their judgmental attitudes and pious platitudes only furthered Job's pain. In utter frustration he responded, "But ask the animals, or the birds . . . or . . . the earth, or let the fish of the sea inform you." Job had seen the wicked prosper and mock God while the righteous suffered in pain. Yet, Job had seen something else that enabled him to keep trusting God despite his present circumstances. Job's faith was renewed by observing the perfect order of his Creator's world. In the next few chapters we will do as Job suggested and explore each area of creation he mentioned. I think you'll see why they offer us hope even in times of despair.

Job first suggested we ask the animals. Take the beaver, for example. Beavers are known for their incredible dam-making abilities. Those dams are masterpieces both in their technical engineering as well as their role in the environment. In fact, beavers are the only animals that create entirely new ecosystems. Researchers have determined that the beaver's instinct to build a dam is triggered by the sound of rushing water. Beavers have actually been "tricked" into building dams on dry land just by playing recordings of running water. This shows that these talented engineers are not operating on logic but on a God-given instinct. They are not following written blueprints but rely on the built-in blueprint encoded into their genes. The beaver is a wonderful example of the fine tuned order built into this world by its Maker. If he crafted a beaver with such perfect detail, how can we not trust him with our lives as well!

Nature Journal

12. Designed to Adapt

But ask . . . the birds of the air, and they will tell you . . .
(Job 12:7b)

The Trek:
Read Job 12:7 and Job 39:13-30

Nature Reflections:
Job continued, "the birds of the air . . . will tell you." Not long ago, a Princeton research group studying finches on the Galapagos Islands found that a single year of drought caused their beaks to change. During drought, easily cracked nuts became scarce while the larger, tougher nuts survived. Within a year the finch population had adapted by starting to appear with stronger, wider beaks better designed to break these tougher seeds. These traits were being produced in the entire population of the birds. A few years later the period of drought was replaced by floods and almost immediately, the average finch beak size returned to normal throughout the population. What an amazing feature God placed in the genetic codes of these little creatures that, without a thought or conscious effort on their part, they could develop the subtle physical features necessary to survive changes in their environment.

What could have caused these creatures, with no Princeton education, to be able to produce offspring so perfectly equipped for their new environment? It all took place almost as if the little birds were programmed to survive. But then, they were, weren't they! As Job asked, "Which of all these does not know that the hand of the LORD has done this? While the adaptability of the Galapagos finches is amazing, the point Job was making is even more amazing. Job was going through a time of indescribable suffering but he knew that the life of every living thing, including his own, is safe in its Creator's hands. If God is able to design finches that can adapt to their changing environment, we can be assured that he will give each of his beloved children all that we need to get through even the most impossible looking circumstances.

Nature Journal

13. The Earth will Teach You

. . . or speak to the earth, and it will teach you.
(Job 12:8a)

The Trek:
Read Job 12:7-8 and Job 38

Nature Reflections:

Job continued his admonition by telling his friends to learn from the earth. In my High School environmental biology class we spent as much time learning about the environment outside as we did in the classroom. One time after a quick stop at the swamp, we came back to examine our buckets of mud under the microscope. Every sample we viewed was teeming with living organisms. Life on this planet is ubiquitous. As Job had suggested, the earth is permeated with living creatures whose existence testifies to the One from whom all life has come. In addition to life itself, even the earth's amazing ability to sustain such life points to a designer. It is an ongoing demonstration of such order, precision, and detail it could only have been designed by the hands of a Chief Engineer. The earth's hydrological cycle, for example, is a continually self-sustaining wonder of clouds and rain, condensation, precipitation and evaporation that keeps the earth watered and able to maintain life. The system is so finely tuned and energy-efficient that the USDA states, "The water cycle prevails in all places and at all times with neither beginning nor end." That description is not only amazing but sounds a lot like a description of the Master Architect, himself.

Yes, Job was right when he told his friends to look at the earth and let it teach them a thing or two about their Creator. Its endless supply of natural wonders and living creatures along with its built-in ability to support that life offers all the proof we need to believe in a Master Designer. And in that proof, we are also reassured that no matter how difficult our present situation might be, the system is designed to ultimately work out for the best in the end.

Nature Journal

14. The Fish Will Inform You

. . . or let the fish of the sea inform you.
(Job 12:8b)

The Trek:
Read Job 12:7-8 and Job 41

Nature Reflections:
Job concluded his admonition by suggesting his friends could learn something about life by studying the aquatic world. The migratory cycle of the salmon family is remarkably specific, with each generation returning to spawn in the exact same place as the generation before it. The Atlantic salmon migrates to fresh water in late spring swimming upstream at up to four miles per day. Because salmon can jump up to 12 feet out of water, they can clear almost any obstacle in their path. The female lays her eggs in the fall and then the adult salmon make the return trip back downstream to the sea. The Atlantic salmon does not die after it spawns but returns every year to its breeding place. The North Pacific Salmon spawn only once and then die after depositing and fertilizing their eggs. The Chinook salmon migrates farther than the others often traveling up to 2000 miles inland to its spawning ground.

What could account for this kind of internal drive that enables these mighty creatures to travel such long distances with such flawless accuracy? Only a Master Designer could devise such a mechanism for the continuation of life. And doesn't the word, "mechanism" itself, imply a Mechanic? So, as Job concludes his little verbal tour of the natural world —the animals, birds, earth and sea—he asks, "Which of all these does not know that the hand of the LORD has done this?" Those who would ask where God is in their darkest hours, need only look at the world he created for their answer. As they observe its beauty and its perfect order they can be reminded that he is in control even now and that he can be trusted to see them safely through the darkness and into His glorious light.

Nature Journal

15. Fingerprints

When I consider your heavens, the work of your fingers, the moon and the stars, which you have set in place, what is man that you are mindful of him, the son of man that you care for him?

(Ps. 8:3, 4)

The Trek:
Read Psalm 8

Nature Reflections:
"It's like looking at God!" It could have been me uttering these words as I gazed into a crystal clear, star-filled night sky. Yes, it could easily have been me but it was not. These words were spoken by an astronomer after one of his experiments proved successful. George Smoot, an astrophysicist at the University of California at Berkeley, is the project leader for the Cosmic Background Explorer (COBE) space project that was, at the time, attempting to prove the theory that the universe had a beginning in time (as opposed to an eternal existence). In April of 1992, COBE transmitted a report revealing, almost precisely, the predicted measurements needed to confirm his theory. When it did, Smoot's response was to declare, "What we have found is evidence for the birth

of the universe." Headlines all over the world quoted him saying, "If one is religious, it's like looking at God."

When asked about this now famous statement Dr. Smoot (not generally known to be a religious person) explained, "Not only did we find what are the seeds of the modern day structure . . . but we also found evidence of the birth of the universe. . . so it's really like looking back at creation and seeing the creation of space and time and the universe and everything in it, but also. . . the fingerprints from the Maker." When the Psalmist described the marvels of creation or, as he called them, "the works of your fingers," his response was one of awe ("what is man that you . . . care for him?") and worship ("Oh LORD, our Lord, how majestic is your name in all the earth!"). The Lord created this glorious Universe with us in mind, and it gives him great delight when our response is to give all the glory to him.

Nature Journal

16. David's Deer

He makes my feet like the feet of a deer;
he enables me to stand on the heights.
(Ps. 18:33)

The Trek:
Read Psalm 18:28-50

Nature Reflections:

I went down to the bay to pick water lilies. As I was reaching to grasp the closest flower I noticed a slight motion. I almost gasped out loud when I looked up and saw a magnificent buck drinking from the water just across the bay. It was almost like watching a reenactment of David's Psalm 42: "As the deer pants for streams of water, so my soul pants for you, O God." My foot slipped and, to avoid falling into the water, I had to shift positions causing the mighty beast to disappear into the woods with the flash of his white tail. It is that white tail or "flag" that gives the white-tailed deer its name. No matter how many times I spot a deer in motion I am awed. From his writings it appears that David the Psalmist must have felt the same way about these graceful creatures.

David spent most of his early years as a shepherd boy, tending his flocks. It was most likely there, in the wilds, that he had seen flocks of deer bounding up the craggy hills. Despite the rugged terrain these agile creatures reached the top of the peaks effortlessly. So it was only natural that David would write, "He makes my feet like the feet of a deer" to illustrate how God had enabled him to escape the many enemies he had who sought his life. Through it all, David continued to trust in his God to deliver him, and faithful to His word, God did. In response to his miraculous deliverance David penned those picturesque words as a song of victory and thanksgiving. God had enabled David to "stand on the heights." He will do the same for all who trust him to keep them from falling.

Nature Journal

17. Hurting and Broken

The LORD is close to the brokenhearted and
saves those who are crushed in spirit.
(Ps. 34:18)

The Trek:
Read Psalm 34

Nature Reflections:
My mom was always bringing home wounded animals.
For as long as I can remember, our house was a refuge and
urgent care facility for any injured creature that came across
her path. She took in sick bunnies, stray dogs, birds with broken wings, and even a turtle with a damaged shell. Having no
formal veterinary training, mom used the materials at hand,
home remedies, and lots of tender loving care. Not all of the
creatures survived, but she nurtured enough of them back to
health to keep her willing to take on the next sick critter case
that came along. Back then, I thought it was great fun getting
to watch these wounded creatures be treated and released
back into the wild (except the stray dog—we kept him!).
Looking back now, I realize I was receiving a far greater education than animal care.

Today, I better understand what motivated my mom to look after sick creatures. As a child, my mom had never fully experienced the love that a child needs to grow emotionally strong and secure. Now we all know stories of abused children who ended up being bitter and hateful adults. What happened to my mom was just the opposite. As a young adult, she had a personal encounter with the God of love. She was so totally transformed by his healing touch that she became filled with compassion and the desire to reach out to all who are suffering as she once had. Her caring ranged everywhere from wounded turtles to hurting people. The new heart mom had been given was nothing less than the loving heart of God, himself, reaching out to others through her. Yes, God has a special place in His heart for the hurting and broken—and for you!

Nature Journal

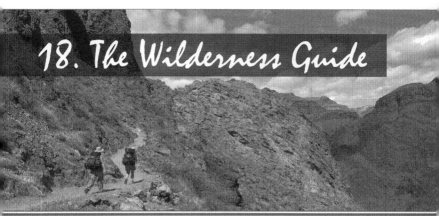

18. The Wilderness Guide

Photo courtesy NPS

For this God is our God for ever and ever;
he will be our guide even to the end.
(Ps 48:14)

The Trek:
Read Psalm 48

Nature Reflections:

Our new Chairman arrived a little late. That's because he also moonlights as a professional wilderness guide. His start date had to be set for after his guided tour of Alaska. Fortunately for us, he and his entire group all returned safely and we got our long awaited Chairman. There are numerous reasons one should consider hiring a professional guide for exploring the great outdoors. Guides offer a safe, enjoyable and exciting way to travel to remote areas. They can provide such opportunities as nature studies, white water activities, rock climbing and numerous winter sports. In addition, experienced guides can save you the pitfalls of learning by trial and error and can help you know where to go as well as where *not* to go. Most importantly, a professional guide can assure that at the end of your adventure, you will get back home safely.

Let's face it. Life is a lot like taking a wilderness excursion. There are numerous pitfalls along the way and it is very easy to take a wrong path and find oneself completely lost. That is why God never intended us to make the journey on our own. Anyone who tries to tackle life's challenges in their own strength is just as foolish as the inexperienced adventurer who heads into the woods without a professional guide. God has offered every one of us our own personal wilderness guide and he has even offered to pick up the tab. Through his Spirit living within us he will be with us every step of the way. He will show us where to go, and where not to go. Best of all, he has given us his professional guarantee and will see to it personally that at the end of our travels we will safely arrive Home.

Nature Journal

19. Cattle Call

For every animal of the forest is mine,
and the cattle on a thousand hills.
(Ps. 50:10)

The Trek:
Read Psalm 50

Nature Reflections:

Bob and I had gone for a walk through a large State Forest. We spotted a clearing ahead of us and arrived at a barbed wire fence. As we did, about 50 heads popped up. A herd of cows had been grazing just beyond the fence. They looked as surprised to see us, as we were to see them. They all stopped eating for the moment and gazed intently at us. "Friends, Romans, Countrymen . . ." Bob suddenly shouted. He had their full attention. "Take me to your leader, earthlings," he continued. They were captivated. Bob continued to orate to the crowd who all appeared to be completely engrossed in the sermon (although I think one or two began to relieve themselves as they listened). When Bob had completed his message (and I stopped laughing) we left our attentive audience who went back to grazing, no worse for the encounter.

We have often thought about our cattle congregation. They reminded us of some churches we've visited where the pastor pours his heart out to an audience who appears completely unaffected by the message. Or, as Timothy put it, they are "always learning but never able to acknowledge the truth" (2 Tim. 3:7). God wants us to be both hearers and doers of the Word. It's easy just to sit back and take in knowledge, to nod our heads to apparent truths but then to walk away and remain untouched, unchanged. We can be like the gracious cows who politely accepted everything Bob preached to them that day and then went back to their grazing. Or, we can choose to internalize, and then act upon the truths we hear. For the man who, "not forgetting what he has heard, but doing it—he will be blessed in what he does" (James 1:25).

Nature Journal

20. First Snow

Cleanse me with hyssop, and I will be clean;
wash me, and I will be whiter than snow.
(Ps. 51:7)

The Trek:
Read Psalm 51

Nature Reflections:

The world had turned gray! It was late fall and any leaves remaining on the trees had lost every trace of color. The sky was blanketed by dark stratus clouds making the scene all the more gray and colorless. I was starting to feel a bit gray, myself so I went inside and looked at some color pictures. After a while, Bob came running into the room and, with great bravado, announced, "First Snow!" We had been married long enough for me to understand the monumental significance of the occasion. So, I came to the window with him. Sure enough, those ominous clouds were now releasing puffy white flakes of snow. I looked over and saw Bob's eyes dancing with enthusiasm. "First snow" had been an exciting annual event for him and his brothers since childhood. A friend of their family even used to mark the date right on the wall each year, to the kids' delight (who, of course, had been taught *not* to write on walls).

After victoriously making his mark in the appropriate place (*not* on the wall), we stood at the window and watched as the once dreary gray world was transformed into a brilliant white masterpiece. I thought of the verses, "Therefore, if anyone is in Christ, he is a new creation; the old has gone, the new has come!" (2 Cor. 5:17). What the first snow had done to a colorless world beautifully portrays what the Lord does to a life surrendered to his loving care— he makes us whiter than snow. By the way, Bob isn't the only one who likes to celebrate First Snow. Every time someone gives their heart to Jesus, he turns a life that was once soiled by sin from grayness to white, and all of Heaven rejoices.

Nature Journal

21. Call of the Wild

Then my enemies will turn back when I call for help.
By this I will know that God is for me.
(Ps 56:9)

The Trek:
Read Psalm 56

Nature Reflections:

Even though I was only about 10 years old I remember it as
if it were yesterday. We were on vacation in Canada. It was
a peaceful summer evening and we sat by the lake watching
the steady parade of fishing boats coming in for the night.
Suddenly, the peace was broken by what sounded like the
hysterical cries of a loon. We ran to the water's edge and
saw a small outboard boat chasing a loon in circles. The bird
seemed utterly distraught and its terrified cries could be
heard for miles. We wondered why the loon didn't just take
off and escape its attacker. Perhaps it was injured. We looked
on in horror as the driver of the small craft seemed to be
taking pleasure in tormenting the helpless creature. Eventually, the loon managed to fly away to safety. I had secretly
hoped the boater got swallowed by a sea monster on the way
home. I later learned the bird was probably trying to protect

its nesting young. Her wild calls were merely a distraction intended to lure the perceived attacker far enough away from the nest to be of any danger.

I will never forget the sound of the loon being chased that night. But knowing what I do now, makes the memory all the more meaningful. That mother loon was putting her life on the line for her young. God gave the loon this amazing instinct to use her hysterical sounding cries so her chicks would be safe. God wants us humans to cry out in our times of distress as well. But in our case, it was God, himself, who put his life on the line. He took all of the punishment meant for us, upon himself at the Cross so that when we need his help, help is just one cry away.

Nature Journal

22. Under His Wings

. . . I think of you through the watches of the night. Because you are my help, I sing in the shadow of your wings.
(Ps 63:6, 7)

The Trek:
Read Psalm 63

Nature Reflections:
Ironsides Island is a New York State protected bird sanctuary, located directly across from our camp. For many years the herons have taken the State up on its offer and built their nests by the hundreds in its treetops. The Great Blue Heron is appropriately named standing up to 52 inches tall, with a wing span of over 5 feet. Like the other members of the Long Legged Wader family, it is a tall bird with a long neck and stilt-like legs. It is a social bird that nests in colonies. The birds arrive in early spring, lay their eggs, and the chicks hatch about a month later. At least one adult will remain at the nest almost constantly. The male watches the nest during the day while the female hunts for food, and the roles are reversed at night until the young ones are able to head out on their own.

From our vantage point on shore we get to see and hear it all. During the day, the sky is filled with a steady stream of herons making their reconnaissance flights to the shore for food. At night, the island sounds more like a jungle as the nesting herons begin to cackle so loud you can hear them for miles. I wonder if it is significant that the females have nest duty at night. We girls are known for being talkative. Or, just perhaps, it is a heron praise concert. Either way, all those giant birds sitting vigilantly on their nests, day and night, through good weather and bad, paint a picture similar to one used repeatedly in the Scriptures to describe the nurturing, attentive, protective stance of our Savior over each of his children. There is no place on earth safer than under his wings.

Nature Journal

22. Mike

Hear me, O God, as I voice my complaint; protect my life from the threat of the enemy. Hide me from the conspiracy of the wicked, from that noisy crowd of evildoers.
(Ps. 64:1, 2)

The Trek:
Read Psalm 64

Nature Reflections:
They would put Arthur Murray to shame with their fancy footwork. Bob and I discovered one night that we had an entire dance troupe using our backyard as their own private studio. It had snowed that day and the ground was completely blanketed in white. Before going to bed I flipped on the back lights for one last look at the fresh snow. To my surprise, there were about a half dozen bunnies all galloping around the yard. The next morning I looked out the window and stared in amazement. The entire yard was covered with bunny tracks. They must have had an all night bunny dance marathon. Now, as much as I appreciate wildlife, I must admit my first thought wasn't one of joy. "There goes the tulips" I thought to myself. I had just planted over 100 bulbs and everyone I knew who had bunnies, had all their tulips eaten to the ground before they

could even bloom. There was nothing I could do at this point but sit back and enjoy the dance.

That spring I was delighted with a yard full of lovely tulips in full bloom. I wondered what had happened to all those dancing (and tulip eating) bunnies until I looked out in the yard one day and saw Mike contentedly strolling through my tulip patch. Mike is the big black cat who lives next door. We quickly learned that Mike rules the land which apparently includes our backyard. I know that without Mike's presence my tulips didn't stand a chance. But the added presence of this one big cat changed the entire backyard dynamic. Remember that next time you must face an overwhelming opponent or challenge. When you invite the Lord into the equation, you win—by an overwhelming majority.

Nature Journal

24. A Mountaintop Experience

Photo by thinkstock.com

The mountains will bring prosperity to the people, the hills the fruit of righteousness.
(Ps 72:3)

The Trek:
Read Psalm 72

Nature Reflections:
When I was invited to attend the special Christian music conference in Colorado I was thrilled. Being with all of those Christian recording artists there in the magnificent foothills of the Rockies gave new meaning to the expression, "a mountaintop experience." As a Christian musician, myself, I admit that thoughts of being "discovered" passed through my mind as I headed to the conference. But that was not the mountaintop experience the Lord had planned for me. I got up early one morning, grabbed my Bible and jogged up one of the nearest hills. As I reached a plateau I stopped and gasped. I stood in a field blazing with yellow wild flowers, completely surrounded by majestic snow capped mountains. I was awed—overwhelmed by the wonder of it all. I fell to ground, pulled out my Bible and had my own private time of prayer and worship right there on the hillside.

I felt God's call on my life in a powerful way that day. Not to a career in Christian music, but to the needy world waiting to hear that the Creator loves them and wants them to personally experience his love. I came down from the mountain renewed and inspired. The following year I had a different kind of mountaintop experience. The Lord allowed me to share my testimony in song at a refugee camp in Austria by the foothills of the Alps. My trip gave new meaning to Isaiah's words, "How beautiful on the mountains are the feet of those who bring good news, who proclaim peace, who bring good tidings, who proclaim salvation . . ." (Is 52:7). Having this amazing opportunity was a truly wonderful experience for me. Having a personal relationship with Christ, however, is the only mountaintop experience one never needs to come down from.

Nature Journal

25. The Nocturne

I remembered my songs in the night.
(Ps. 77:6)

The Trek:
Read Psalm 77

Nature Reflections:
"Shhhh! The concert's already begun!" I whispered as Bob slipped quietly into the seat beside me. The sounds flowing through the room were rich and melodic, and I didn't want to miss a single note. This evening's performance was, once again, a beautiful nocturne. The nocturne is a musical composition written to evoke thoughts and feelings of the night. The first composer to use this form was John Field. However, it was Chopin who perfected it and developed it into the style of music recognized worldwide. Well, that's actually not correct. The original nocturne was performed in the Garden of Eden. Since then, its original composer has arranged and produced countless musical scores every night. Bob and I were not sitting in a concert hall, but on the porch listening to a nocturne composed by the Master Creator himself, and the orchestra he was conducting was his nocturnal kingdom—the creatures of the night.

We were enthralled by the twilight performance on this particularly warm summer's eve. As if inspired by the balmy evening breeze, the musicians seemed joyful—almost ecstatic —as they sang. Had I not been concerned about the neighbors questioning my sanity, I would have leapt to my feet and yelled, "bravissimo!" These nightly performers are living witnesses of a Creator who is also a Master Arranger, Composer and Conductor. They also offer a message of encouragement and hope. Most of us will, on occasion, go through times of sorrow in our lives. The songs of the night creatures are a reminder that the concert can go on despite the darkness. Those who keep their eyes fixed on the Master Conductor can keep a perpetual song in their heart even through the darkest of nights because "at night his song is with me" (Psalm 42:8).

Nature Journal

26. A Very Strong Tower

*He who dwells in the shelter of the Most High will
rest in the shadow of the Almighty . . .
He will cover you with his feathers, and
under his wings you will find refuge.*
(Ps. 91:1, 4)

The Trek:
Read Psalm 91

Nature Reflections:

When they saw my reaction, everyone in the room turned
around and looked out the back window. I was sitting at
the piano as the pastor spoke. Mind you, this "church" was
actually located in a castle located on a River island. What
caught my eye was a giant osprey soaring past the chapel
with a giant fish flapping from its claws. The back window
suddenly became more interesting than the morning message and the pastor soon found himself looking at the back
of about 100 heads. Having also seen the osprey he chuckled
and explained that *she* was taking breakfast to a whole nest
of baby ospreys located at the castle's highest peak. Ospreys
are members of the raptor family. They are large birds with
a wingspan of 4 ½ feet. Since they are almost exclusively fish
eaters they commonly live by the water. They build their

bulky nests near the top of large trees, or other tall structures such as power poles, or channel markers. Or, on occasion, a castle roof.

If I was a baby osprey living on the roof of a multimillion dollar castle, I would probably feel quite safe and secure. At least as long as mom was there to provide food and protection. A mother osprey will do just that, defending her young even to her own death. Isn't it interesting, then, that God uses the example of a mighty raptor to describe himself. He, too, willingly gave his life for his people. God also uses the image of a castle: "For you have been my refuge, a strong tower against the foe. I long to . . . take refuge in the shelter of your wings" (Ps 61:3-4). In him, we have the shelter of the gentlest wings, and the security of the strongest tower.

Nature Journal

27. Created to Prey

*You bring darkness, it becomes night,
and all the beasts of the forest prowl. The lions
roar for their prey and seek their food from God.
(Ps. 104:20–21)*

The Trek:
Read Psalm 104:16-35

Nature Reflections:
I had heard there were bobcats in the woods near our camp.
However, it wasn't until I saw one that had been hit by a
car, being held up lengthwise by a wildlife manager, that I
decided to give up taking walks after dark. I suppose I had
previously just thought of them as oversized kitty cats. This
particular one was huge! We must grow them extra large
in the North Country. The bobcat is a member of the lynx
family. It is about twice the size of a domestic cat. A mature
bobcat is about two feet tall and averages 36 inches in length
including its (of course) bobbed tail. Bobcats are mainly nocturnal and come well equipped for the night with their large
eyes that are easily adapted to see in the dark and slit-shaped
pupils that can open wide to admit light. They have retract-
able hooked claws and four large canine teeth. In addition,

they have a sharp sense of hearing and smell to match their night vision. In combination, this makes bobcats excellent hunters. They stalk their prey with stealth and then capture it, with one great leap.

Bobcats have been perfectly designed to go out into the night and hunt down what they need to eat in order to survive. One might say they were created to prey. We humans, on the other hand, were created to *pray*. God has perfectly designed us with both the ability and the need to communicate with our Creator. Pouring our hearts out to him in prayer helps us face each day with confidence and assures us we will also make it through even the darkest nights (no matter how many bobcats there are, out there!). So while the bobcats are out preying, you'll find me inside, praying!

Nature Journal

28. There All Along

The LORD is near to all who call on him, to all who call on him in truth. He fulfills the desires of those who fear him; he hears their cry and saves them. (Ps. 145:18, 19)

The Trek:
Read Psalm 145

Nature Reflections:
First we saw the deer. Then, we saw the camper speed around the corner. At the last minute the deer leaped out of the path of danger. But as the vehicle tore on past, I saw something else out of the corner of my eye. When we got to the spot we discovered, to our horror, the body of a tiny fawn crumpled at the side of the road. Bob went over and tenderly touched the limp form. Suddenly, the fawn lifted its head and gave a startlingly loud cry. "Maaaaaah!" He was calling for his mother. The fawn had a large, bleeding gash on his head and was clearly dazed and disoriented. The fawn looked up at Bob and cried again, this time much weaker, "Maaaah!" We stood there helplessly wondering what to do when we heard a loud snorting sound in the brush just a few feet from us.

When she started to stomp her feet, we decided it was time to exit. We watched from a distance as the two were reunited. A few days later, mother and fawn were walking through the woods together (and hopefully avoiding the highway).

Some of our Lord's attributes are demonstrated in how this mother deer cared for her wounded fawn. While we were wondering where the mother had gone, she was there all along keeping a watchful eye over her baby. And when she heard its cry of distress, she was there at its side licking its bleeding wounds, helping it get back on its feet, and nurturing it back to full health. When life knocks you down and you find yourself wondering where God was in your time of crisis, remember the little fawn and cry out to your Heavenly Father. He has been there all along.

Nature Journal

29. Praise Concert

*Praise him, you highest heavens and you waters above
the skies. Let them praise the name of the LORD,
for he commanded and they were created.*
(Ps. 148:4, 5)

The Trek:
Read Psalm 148

Nature Reflections:
I looked out the window longingly. The brilliant blue sky and
puffy white cumulus clouds were beckoning me to come out
and play. I looked around me and noticed most of my co-
workers also sneaking some longing glances out the window.
Somehow, we all made it to 5:00 PM (or was it 4:59?) before
bolting for the door. In one big blur I was out the door, into
my car, driving through the rush hour traffic (it seemed like
a lot of us were hurrying out of town that day) and finally
arrived home. By 6:00 PM my kayak and I had launched from
shore and were headed to the middle of the lake where I just
sat back and sighed in utter satisfaction. The water pleas-
antly lapped against the boat as the descending sun seemed
to spotlight the green hillside in front of me. All around me,
birds sang, seagulls soared, ducks paddled, and it was as if all

of creation was actively participating in a well coordinated concert of praise.

I have the feeling the Psalmist sat in on a similar worship experience himself when he wrote Psalm 148. He looked into the sky and wrote, "Praise him, sun and moon, praise him, all you shining stars." Then he looked out over the waters and wrote, "Praise the LORD from the earth, you great sea creatures and all ocean depths." There must have been a lovely green hillside in the background as he added, "you mountains and all hills, fruit trees and all cedars" and included the wildlife he saw—the "wild animals and all cattle, small creatures and flying birds." The Psalmist wasn't just observing nature. He was observing nature rendering praise to its Creator. I bet he couldn't help but to join in just like me!

Nature Journal

30. Blowing in the Wind

The wind blows to the south and turns to the north;
round and round it goes, ever returning on its course.
(Eccl 1:6)

The Trek:
Read Ecclesiastes 1:1-6, Solomon 4:10-16

Nature Reflections:

Having grown up around the water I often heard the expression, "Red skies at night, sailor's delight; red in the morning, sailor take warning." Navigators actually do count on the signs in the skies to forecast the coming weather patterns. Still, even those who can read the skies will usually turn to the professionals for the most accurate predictions. Thanks to modern meteorological technology we not only have a fairly accurate idea of what tomorrow's forecast will be, but of the global wind patterns and currents that make up the world's circulation of atmosphere. There are two separate systems involved: the wind, which is the horizontal motion of the atmosphere and; currents, which is motion in a vertical direction. Winds are produced primarily by differences in temperature. When the temperatures of adjacent regions become unequal the warmer air rises and flows over the colder heavier air forming a complex circulation system.

At low levels there is a general drift of air toward the equator while at the upper levels another drift toward the poles completes the cyclical pattern.

Only a few centuries ago mankind had no concept of a worldwide atmospheric cycle. It is interesting to note that because the technology has only recently existed, the world's patterns of winds could not have been understood at the time the Bible was written. Nor could they have realized the movement of air was the result of changes of atmospheric pressure traveling in an eternal north-south circulation. Solomon, the author of Ecclesiastes did not have a Doppler radar to view the circulation of atmosphere when he wrote that "the wind blows to the south and turns to the north; round and round it goes." What he clearly did have was the inspiration of the One who put the system in place.

Nature Journal

31. Current Events

*All streams flow into the sea, yet the sea
is never full. To the place the streams
come from, there they return again.*
(Eccl 1:7)

The Trek:
Read Ecclesiastes 1:7-18, Psalm 135:1-7

Nature Reflections:
I climbed down the long flight of stairs below the Thousand
Islands Bridge with my inflatable life raft in hand. The islands
are so tightly clumped together in this lovely spot on the
River that I figured it would be easy to row in and among
them. It wasn't quite as easy as I had imagined. I pushed off
from land and almost immediately found myself heading
back toward shore. Just as quickly, I was spun around again
and was sent in another direction. My little boat was being
carried along in the River currents. What I encountered that
day is insignificant compared to the oceanic currents that
make up the earth's circulation of atmosphere. The inten-
sity and direction of each weather pattern is dramatically
affected as it passes over the sea. The waters actually dictate
what those weather patterns will be. So, while sailors are concerned about how the weather will affect their travel on the

ocean, ultimately it is the ocean and its currents that affect the weather.

The ocean currents are kept in constant motion by prevailing winds. The best known ocean current is the Gulf Stream in the North Atlantic which flows northeast from Florida to Newfoundland. Its sources are two equatorial currents. Scientists have recently discovered that the turbulence produced by these opposing currents produce massive storms beneath the surface of the ocean and play a significant role in global atmospheric circulation. Interestingly, the Psalmist described the oceanic paths long ago when he wrote about "the fish of the sea, all that swim the paths of the seas" (Ps. 8:8). The authors of the Scriptures had their meteorology right because they were writing under the inspiration of the One of whom it was written, "Even the wind and the waves obey Him!" (Mk. 4:38-41).

Nature Journal

Photo courtesy USFWS

32. White Christmas

*The people walking in darkness have seen a
great light; on those living in the land of
the shadow of death a light has dawned
. . . For to us a child is born, to us a son is given . . .
And he will be called Wonderful Counselor, Mighty
God, Everlasting Father, Prince of Peace.*
(Is. 9:2, 6)

The Trek:

Read Isaiah 8:17 - 9:7

Nature Reflections:

Never mind Christmas. Here in Upstate, New York, white
Thanksgivings, white Easters, and even an occasional white
Mother's Day aren't all that uncommon. I remember one
year, however, that was different. The snow didn't come!
October passed, then November, but once we hit December
still with no significant snowfall, we all started singing a different tune (you guessed it: "White Christmas"). Then, just
a week before Christmas, I woke up to a world blanketed
in white. A fluffy white snow had fallen overnight covering
not only the drab gray ground, but every tree branch, every
phone wire, and even every needle on the evergreens. It was

like waking up to a wintery fantasy land. I ran outdoors to experience the wonder and as I did, the sun came out from behind the lingering clouds. Suddenly, the already white scene took on a brilliance that was almost too dazzling for my eyes to handle. It looked like we'd be having that white Christmas after all.

Now, I realize many people have never had the opportunity to experience the kind of white Christmas we have here in the North. I spent one Christmas in Florida where the only white I saw was the lights hanging from the palm trees. But as I gazed at those white lights I was reminded there is a lot more about Christmas that makes it a white holiday than snowfall. The Bible describes the birth of Christ saying, "The true light that gives light to every man was coming into the world" (John 1:9). Jesus was the Light in a world darkened by evil. He came to make us whiter than snow. So, wherever you happen to be celebrating this year, thank God for sending us the Light of the World, and have a white Christmas.

Nature Journal

33. Falling Stars

Photo by Ed Sweeney

How have you fallen from heaven. O morning star, son of the dawn! You have been cast down to the earth, you who once laid low the nations!

(Is. 14:12)

The Trek:
Read Isaiah 14:1-15

Nature Reflections:
They had been predicting it for months so we were well aware that the meteor shower of a lifetime would be taking place that very night. I set my alarm but was wide awake just before 3:00 AM, the time it was supposed to peak. Sure enough, the night sky was alive with a continuous display of lights as meteors streamed across the horizon. To the naked eye, meteors appear as fast moving streaks of light which is why they are often referred to as falling or shooting stars. They are not really stars at all. Meteoroids are tiny sand-sized particles that orbit the sun that usually can't be seen. The meteoroids only become visible when they enter the Earth's atmosphere. At that point they are referred to as meteors. They become visible because of the friction caused by striking air molecules at which point the meteors start to flow in blue or white. Most meteors burn up in the atmosphere.

Occasionally a larger meteor (referred to as a meteorite) will fall to the earth's surface.

The Bible uses the illustration of a shooting star to describe the rebellious angel Lucifer being thrown down from his heavenly position. For a time, God has allowed this once glorious creature to enter earth's atmosphere and fall to its surface. But never forget that though he retains the appearance of power and light, Satan has already been defeated. It is just a matter of time until his strength is burned up and his evil light snuffed out once and for all. In the mean time, we can wait out the meteor storm under the protective cover of God's grace. There is no place more secure than in the mighty arms of the One who has already won the victory for his people.

Nature Journal

34. As the Deer

*Then will the lame leap like a deer, and the mute
tongue shout for joy. Water will gush forth
in the wilderness and streams in the desert
(Is. 35:6)*

The Trek:
Read Isaiah 35

Nature Reflections:
I was out for an early morning jog. As I came around the
bend, I came to an abrupt halt. There, standing less than
50 feet away from me, was a mother deer with her tiny spotted fawn. The instant I came into view both heads popped
up and froze in a startled stare. For the next several magical
moments the three of us stood motionlessly gazing at each
other. Our moment came to an abrupt end when a car came
down the road and broke the spell. The next thing I saw was
a flash of white as mother and fawn bounded away in perfect
synchrony. Typically, a doe gives birth to twin fawns. For the
first few months they are well camouflaged by hundreds of
white spots on their reddish-brown coats. The spots gradually disappear and by winter they are completely gone. When

my two deer were completely gone, I happily continued my jog humming one of my favorite choruses, "As the Deer."

The deer is used in the Bible to illustrate grace and beauty, as well as strength and victory. As the deer springs effortlessly to the top of every hill in its path, so too, the child of God has been promised strength and grace sufficient to tackle every trial and hardship we encounter along the way. But when Isaiah spoke of the lame leaping like a deer he was describing the Lord's return to earth. On that day he will put an end to all pain, suffering, and even death. Jesus, the Messiah, will come and defeat Satan, bringing deliverance, healing, and above all, joy to all who have put their trust in him. The future that awaits us, as described so eloquently by Isaiah, will give us every reason to leap for joy.

Nature Journal

35. Thermal Dynamics

> *. . . but those who hope in the LORD will renew their strength. They will soar on wings like eagles; they will run and not grow weary, they will walk and not be faint*
> *(Is. 40:31)*

The Trek:

Read Isaiah 40:21–31

Nature Reflections:

After the terrorist attacks upon the United States on September 11, 2001, a picture began to circulate of a crying eagle. The eagle first became the national emblem in 1782 when the Continental Congress adopted the current design for the Great Seal of the United States. The eagle was selected by the founding fathers because it is a species unique to North America and because it symbolized strength, courage, and freedom. The seal depicts a Bald Eagle supporting a shield composed of 13 red and white stripes representing the thirteen original states with a scroll in his beak inscribed, "E Pluribus Unum" ("out of many, one"). It is grasping thirteen arrows in one talon and a thirteen-leaf olive branch in the other. Note that the eagle faces the olive branch. On September 11th, the US Eagle cried.

An eagle's wings are long and broad—custom designed for soaring. To help them soar, eagles use thermals, or rising currents of warm air. With the help of thermals, soaring requires a minimum amount of wing flapping. They also aid them in long migrational flights as they climb high in a thermal and then glide downward to catch the next. Using this method, an eagle can travel great distances almost effortlessly. The Bible uses the symbol of the eagle to describe those who put their confidence in the Lord. By the power of His Spirit working within us we can soar almost effortlessly. Even through such tragedies as what took place on September 11th. Speaking of thermals, the Greek word used for the Holy Spirit, "Pneuma" also means wind.* God doesn't ask us to soar through the rough times on our own. He has provided the wind of his Spirit to enable us to rise above even our most difficult situations.

* see John 3:8

Nature Journal

36. A Far Stretch

Photo by European Southern Observatory (ESO)

*This is what the LORD says—your Redeemer,
who formed you in the womb: I am the LORD,
who has made all things, who alone stretched out
the heavens, who spread out the earth by myself.*
(Is 44:24)

The Trek:

Read Isaiah 44:6-24

Nature Reflections:

"Is it something we said?" was my smart aleck answer when I first heard that all of the galaxies in the universe are retreating from the earth at a very high rate of speed. Astronomer Edwin Hubble confirmed this in 1929 and also found that the more distant galaxies are retreating at a faster rate than the nearer ones, all of which confirms that our universe is expanding. If it is expanding, that points to a universe with a beginning. And if the universe had a beginning, one can only conclude it had a Beginner or Creator. We now know that the universe has been expanding at the precise rate of speed needed to allow for life as we know it here on earth. The tiniest rate variance in either direction would have upset the balance needed to sustain life. This perfect balance is yet another example of the minutely detailed blueprints of a Master Designer.

While the expanding universe is considered a discovery of the 20th century, the Bible has stated this all along. Jeremiah wrote, "God made the earth by his power . . . and stretched out the heavens by his understanding" (Jer 10:12) As astounding as that is, there is another stretch God made that was even more amazing. His farthest stretch wasn't to expand a universe but in reaching from beyond its outermost limits to the hearts of mankind. He declared, "I will redeem you with an outstretched arm . . ." (Ex. 6:6). He has reached out to every individual "with a mighty hand and outstretched arm; His love endures forever" (Ps. 136:12). God has extended his loving hand across the insurmountable distance that exists between a holy God and the people he formed in his image to love. Because he did, he is just a single prayer away.

Nature Journal

37. Mother Earth or Father God?

For this is what the LORD says—he who created the heavens, he is God; he who fashioned and made the earth, he founded it; he did not create it to be empty, but formed it to be inhabited—he says: "I am the LORD, and there is no other."

(Is. 45:18)

The Trek:

Read Isaiah 45:5-21

Nature Reflections:

"Save the whales!" "I brake for animals." "Be good to your Mother earth!" We've all seen such bumper stickers expressing the heartfelt sentiments of those who are passionate about protecting the environment. It would seem that we as believers should be on the forefront of this movement if we take seriously the commission God gave us to care for the earth. Instead, we often find ourselves at odds with some of the groups that claim to be saving the planet. Though admittedly, some of them are motivated by an entirely different belief system than we are, rejecting even the existence of a Divine Creator. Some, instead, believe that the natural world is all there is. We are all here by chance and if we don't "care for our Mother Earth" we could destroy this fragile, coincidentally life-sustaining planet. People who believe this are, essentially, worshiping the creation rather than the Creator. Ironically, that means they are attempting to save the natural world they worship.

Yet, if mankind can't save mother earth, there is no reason to think Mother Earth can offer salvation to mankind. Thankfully, God can. While some are trying desperately to save the earth, we know that our Creator is its Sustainer as well. We are told, "For by him all things were created: things in heaven and on earth . . . and in him all things hold together" (Col 1:16,17). Yes, we have a God-given responsibility to care for the earth and its creatures but we are working directly under the tutelage and supreme control of the One who has promised, "Turn to me and be saved, all you ends of the earth; for I am God, and there is no other" (Is. 45:22). Yes, I brake for animals, too, and I think my Father is pleased.

Nature Journal

38. Peaceable Kingdom

Peaceable Kingdom, c. 1834, Edward Hicks, National Gallery of Art

*"The wolf and the lamb will feed together, and the
lion will eat straw like the ox, but dust will be the
serpent's food. They will neither harm nor destroy
on all my holy mountain," says the LORD.*

(Is. 65:25)

The Trek:
Read Isaiah 65

Nature Reflections:

The first time it happened, I was sound asleep. Or, at least I
had been sound asleep. I grumpily called out to my husband
and told him to turn down the TV. It sounded like some old
western movie complete with wild animal sounds. Bob let
me know that the TV wasn't even on. Then I heard it again
and realized the sound was coming from outside. Bob came
and joined me, and for the next 10 minutes or so, we listened
to howls and shrieks that ran chills up our spines. I had seen
enough nature movies to know we were hearing the sound
of coyotes. After a while the noise subsided and we admitted
being thankful for listening from inside the camp. The coyote is a member of the canine family which includes wolves,
dogs and foxes. They range anywhere from 20 to over 50
pounds, with the biggest ones being common to our area.

There is some speculation, and even some evidence that our 50 pound coyotes are actually hybridized from coyotes and Algonquin wolves.

The thought of roving packs of wolves running around in our backyard makes me a little less likely to go out for an evening jog. The Bible speaks of a day, however, when all of that will change. Isaiah writes, "Behold, I will create new heavens and a new earth . . . be glad and rejoice forever in what I will create" (Is. 65:17-17). Not only will there be peace in the animal kingdom but all of humankind as well. We will lay down all of our arms and instead worship our Savior with our arms uplifted in praise. So for now, we'll enjoy the coyote concerts from indoors knowing one day we'll be singing right alongside them in God's new peaceable kingdom.

Nature Journal

39. Peace Like A River

*For this is what the LORD says: "I will extend
peace to her like a river, and the wealth
of nations like a flooding stream.
(Is. 66:12)*

The Trek:
Read Isaiah 66

Nature Reflections:
We had to get up before sunrise and drive two hours to a
funeral. It is always sad to lose a loved one but it was particularly painful seeing the deep grief of the family members left
behind. We did our best to offer our love and support and
then started the four hour trip back. Yes, four! We were not
headed home but for the River. Emotionally drained and
physically exhausted we arrived at camp just moments before
sunset. Without even unpacking the car I ran to my favorite
bench and remained there for the next hour. As the setting
sun slipped behind the hills, I felt the pressures of the day
passing away with it. I gazed at the brilliant pink sky mirrored
in the tranquil waters and whispered a weary, 'Thank you,
Lord." For the first time that day I felt completely engulfed in

his peace. The old hymn, "Peace Like A River" came to mind along with the passage in Isaiah where it was taken from.

Is it a stretch to read so much symbolism into nature? Not unless one were to accuse the Author, himself, of doing the same. The Bible is rich with illustrations using objects of creation. Perhaps a better question to ask is whether God originally built those attributes into his Creation for the express purpose of using them as illustrations to us. To create such an amazingly beautiful world that could evoke such emotions indicates to me that he had us in mind even before creating us. Made in his own image, he gave us the unique ability to appreciate and feel the excitement, exhilaration, and awe over the works of his hands. We, alone, can enjoy the wonder of his creation and experience peace like a river.

Nature Journal

40. Fear of Water

O LORD, the hope of Israel, all who forsake you will be put to shame. Those who turn away from you will be written in the dust because they have forsaken the LORD, the spring of living water.
(Jer. 2:13)

The Trek:
Read Jeremiah 2:1-22

Nature Reflections:

It was well past sunset but I couldn't pull myself away from its gracefully ebbing glow. Out of the corner of my eye, a slight motion snapped me out of my blissful gaze. A large fox was awkwardly wandering through the bushes. The creature looked disoriented and was acting strangely. Knowing of the existence of rabies in our area, I decided it was time to head inside to the safety of our cottage. As I made my way across the yard, the fox spotted me and, rather than running away, began to slowly move toward me. As the door to safety closed behind me I looked out into the now nearly dark yard and watched the obviously sick animal stagger off into the night. The next morning we found him dead at the side of the road. He had apparently strayed into the path of an oncoming car and was put out of his misery.

Rabies is a viral disease that affects the nervous system. It is transmitted from infected mammals to man and is fatal once symptoms appear. Its scientific name, hydrophobia, literally means "fear of water." One of the symptoms is constriction of the throat muscles causing the animal to foam at the mouth, and be unable to swallow. Once the disease has progressed to this point death is imminent. There is a spiritual form of hydrophobia that is equally fatal if left untreated. The Scriptures refer to the Lord as the spring of living water. Jesus promised, "Indeed, the water I give . . . will become in him a spring of water welling up to eternal life" (John 4:14). Running from the source of living water will leave one stumbling helplessly in the dark. So, why not come to the living, healing water and drink freely today.

Nature Journal

41. Memories

"No longer will a man teach his neighbor, or a man his brother, saying, Know the LORD, because they will all know me, from the least of them to the greatest," declares the LORD. "For I will forgive their wickedness and will remember their sins no more."
(Jer. 31:34)

The Trek:
Read Jeremiah 31:31-40

Nature Reflections:
It's easy to train a wild chickadee to eat from your hand. I started by standing near the bird feeder with my extended hand full of seeds. Once they grew accustomed to my presence I then removed the feeder. It didn't take long before I had my first customer. A single chick zipped down and landed just long enough to snatch up a seed and fly away. He must have shared the news with his friends because it wasn't long until I had a steady stream of chickadees landing on my hand, grabbing a seed, and zipping away. I might have taken it personal that they left so abruptly, but that's how chickadees operate. Even at the feeder, they zoom in, grab a seed and fly off to store it away. So, it's not an insult

that they don't stay and eat—it's a survival skill. Another skill God designed these little birds with is an exceptionally good memory by which they are able to remember all the locations where they store their food. This amazing memory enables the chickadee to remember and retrieve food and hence, survive and thrive throughout the winter months.

God has given a special kind of memory to those who put their trust in him. Through the presence of his Spirit in us, we have been given the mind of Christ. He speaks to our hearts and brings his precious Word to mind at the times we need it most. Hence, he enables us to survive and thrive through even our most difficult trials. But God's memory is unique. He who knows all things since the beginning of time, chooses to remember our sins no more when we confess them to him. Now that kind of memory even the chickadees can't compete with.

Nature Journal

42. Sure as the Dawn

*. . . As surely as the sun rises, he will appear; he will
come to us like the winter rains, like the spring rains
that water the earth.*
(Hos. 6:3)

The Trek:
Read Hosea 6

Nature Reflections:
I felt so helpless as my friend shared the heartaches she was
going through. I told her I would pray, and I meant it. But
I wanted to do more. I wanted to somehow reach out and
take away her pain. She smiled and said she just kept trying
to remember, "This, too, shall pass." After we parted, I kept
thinking about her words. Was there really any comfort in
that thought? Does one get through the hard times by simply
believing they will ultimately go away? Is there any guarantee
they *will* go away? But then, the verse came to mind, "Heaven
and earth shall pass away, but my words shall not pass away"
(Mt. 24:35). Yes, our trials will, indeed, pass away. But it is in
what *won't* pass away that we can find our greatest hope and
comfort.

Another common expression is "As sure as the dawn. . ." Hosea used similar words to describe the absolute certainty of God's faithfulness. As sure as the sun rises every morning, we can depend on his loving care. The suffering and pain we experience in this world will eventually come to an end only to be replaced by a far better world—a world without suffering—a world that will never pass away. However, he created the natural world we live in today, along with all of its creatures, to help illustrate that perfect world to come. Every aspect of this present world reveals to us something about his character or his coming kingdom. So, yes, my friend — whatever you are facing today, this, too, shall pass. Sorrow will be replaced with joy, the temporal with the eternal and, best of all, the sun shall be replaced with the Son whose return is as sure as the dawn.

Nature Journal

43. Bugs or Blessings

*Be glad, O people of Zion, rejoice in the LORD
your God, for he has given you the autumn
rains in righteousness. He sends you abundant
showers, both autumn and spring rains, as before.*
(Joel 2:23)

The Trek:
Read Joel 2:21-32

Nature Reflections:

It was a very bad year for locusts. In fact, the crops were completely destroyed. The Prophet Joel used this natural disaster to warn God's rebellious people of his coming judgment. He wrote, "Despair, you farmers . . . because the harvest of the field is destroyed . . . Surely the joy of mankind is withered away" (Joel 1:11-12). Not because of locusts but because "the day of the LORD is coming. It is close at hand—a day of darkness and gloom, a day of clouds and blackness" (Joel 2:1-2). God does not delight in allowing disasters to befall his people but he *does* allow them and, at times he uses them to turn our hearts back to him. He promises, "return to me with all your heart . . . Return to the LORD your God, for he is gracious and compassionate, slow to anger and abounding in love, and he relents from sending calamity" (Joel 2:12-13).

God wants to forgive us, to bless us, and most of all, to enjoy a loving relationship with us. If we return to him with all our hearts, he declares, "I will repay you for the years the locusts have eaten . . . and you will praise the name of the LORD your God, who has worked wonders for you; never again will my people be shamed" (Joel 2:25,26). Joel describes our joyful reunion saying, "In that day the mountains will drip new wine, and the hills will flow with milk; all the ravines of Judah will run with water. A fountain will flow out of the LORD's house and will water the valley of acacias" (Joel 3:18). We can allow our trials to be bugs that destroy us or blessings that draw us closer to the God who desires to pour His love upon us like abundant showers.

Nature Journal

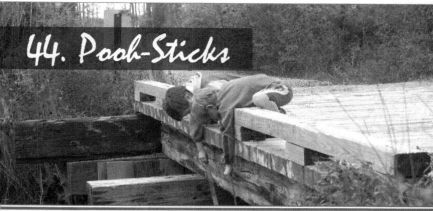

44. Pooh-Sticks

But let justice roll on like a river,
righteousness like a never-failing stream!
(Amos 5:24)

The Trek:
Read Amos 5

Nature Reflections:

It was a game played by the characters in A.A. Milne's *Winnie the Pooh* books. Since it seemed so fun to Piglet and Pooh, my little friends and I would play the game ourselves every time we discovered a bridge crossing a stream. Each player has their own stick. Everyone stands on the upstream side of the bridge and drops their sticks into the water at the same time. Then, we all run to the other side to see whose stick comes out the other side first. After either celebrating our victory or mourning our defeat we would often continue to watch as our sticks slowly continued on down the river to unknown destinations. Maybe even under other bridges. Maybe even with a different outcome. I used to wonder if the real winner should be the one whose stick made it all the way to the end of the creek . . . maybe even out into the ocean.

When Amos compared righteousness to a never-failing stream he must have had the same idea. Anyone, with a little effort, can make it under the first bridge. Maybe they can even get there first. But what matters most in God's eyes is the one who keeps going and faithfully finishes the course. He promised, ". . . you are the branches. If a man remains in me and I in him, he will bear much fruit" (John 15:5). When we commit our lives to him, we become the sticks in his hand, and as Creator of the Universe, you can be sure he always has a winning hand. Oh, and there is a wonderful prize for every winner. Jesus has promised, "To him who overcomes, I will give the right to eat from the tree of life, which is in the paradise of God" (Rev. 2:7).

Nature Journal

45. Oh, Nuts!

*Do not store up for yourselves treasures on earth,
where moth and rust destroy, and where thieves break
in and steal. But store up for yourselves treasures in
heaven, where moth and rust do not destroy,
and where thieves do not break in and steal.*
(Mat 6:19, 20)

The Trek:
Read Matthew 6:1-21

Nature Reflections:
It was mid-December, time to get out our Christmas decorations. I plodded through the snow to our garden house and returned with a box full of lights, wreaths and ornaments. I dumped the contents on the floor. But instead of Christmas ornaments, hundreds of unshelled nuts poured out and rolled in every direction. Somebody had obviously decided my Christmas box was the perfect place to store his winter rations. I remembered seeing a little chipmunk often sitting outside the garden house. When Bob got home and asked why there were nuts all over the floor, I explained my theory. I chuckled and said, "What a disappointment it will be for the little guy when he gets back home to find his entire

winter's provisions completely disappeared, container and all." Bob wouldn't hear of it, and insisted that I immediately put the nuts in the box and take it back out. The chipmunk probably never even noticed they were missing.

Many of us make the same mistake that chipmunk had. We spend our time storing up as many provisions as we can for this life. However, like that box of nuts, all our earthly goods can easily be taken away. That's why God urges us to store up the treasure we can have for eternity. Of course, he wants us to enjoy the blessings he has provided us with here in this life. But when our greatest joy is found in looking forward to spending eternity with him then even if all our earthly possessions were suddenly taken away, our joy remains for "For where your treasure is, there your heart will be also." Our chipmunk's treasure was returned to him. He was fortunate to have Bob looking after him. Thankfully, we have our Heavenly Father looking out for us.

Nature Journal

46. The Hollywood Bird

Look at the birds of the air; they do not sow or reap or store away in barns, and yet your heavenly Father feeds them. Are you not much more valuable than they?
(Mat. 6:26)

The Trek:
Read Matthew 6:22-34

Nature Reflections:

Once autumn has passed and the migratory birds have left for the season, we can still depend on our house finches to keep us company throughout the winter months. While most of the wildlife vacates for the duration of the winter deep freeze, our finch feeder remains a hub of activity for these social little birds. I recently discovered that hadn't always been the case. Prior to 1940, they didn't even exist on the east coast. In 1940, wild birds from the western US began to be sold in New York City by cage-bird dealers who marketed them as "Hollywood Finches." Since selling these wild birds was illegal, the dealers released all their birds on Long Island to avoid prosecution. By 1943 they were reportedly breeding throughout the area. Today, the house finch can be found throughout the US offering their year round companionship and sweet songs.

The profiteers who released the finches in New York City obviously had no concern about the well being and survival of their "merchandise." But by nature of the fact that they not only survived, but thrived, we know that Someone did. God created these and all of his other creatures with the ability to fend for themselves in the natural world he created for them. So, as Jesus said, "Are you not much more valuable than they?" If he cared enough about house finches to enable them to survive a complete change in environment virtually overnight, just think of how much more able and willing he is to help you face every new challenge you encounter! Like the "Hollywood Birds" your ability to get through even your most difficult times is not dependent on others. The Lord, himself, will provide all you need, not just to survive, but to thrive!

Nature Journal

47. Sparrows and Robins

Are not two sparrows sold for a penny? Yet not one of them will fall to the ground apart from the will of your Father . . . So don't be afraid; you are worth more than many sparrows.
(Mat. 10:29, 31)

The Trek:
Read Matthew 10:16-31

Nature Reflections:
I saw the mother robin place the first twigs under the eaves of our deck. From then on, Bob and I watched daily as she completed the nest, laid two blue eggs then sat patiently on her nest for weeks to follow. We arrived home one day to see two fuzzy little wobbling heads. We were enjoying the grandkids immensely until the night of the fierce windstorm. By the next morning, one had fallen from the nest and was struggling on the hard ground below. The other was gone altogether. I called for Bob who came running just as the mother bird arrived on the scene. She flew to her baby and stretched herself across its struggling body but we knew that neither would last very long if they remained there. So Bob put on gloves and gently placed the baby bird back in the nest. But

when the mother returned she went back to the spot on the ground. We could only hope she would return to the nest before it was too late. By sunset, she had not, and the evening chill began to set in.

Needless to say, neither of us got any sleep that night. By morning, the mother bird had found the nest but her baby had not survived the night. We were both in tears as we buried the baby bird, and the verse came to mind, "Yet not one of them will fall to the ground apart from the will of your Father." Surely, if the death of this little bird could break our hearts this much, just think how its Maker must feel. And the point Jesus was making was that if he cares that much about a baby bird, just think about how very much more he cares about you!

Nature Journal

48. Reclaiming the View

The one who received the seed that fell among
the thorns is the man who hears the word, but
the worries of this life and the deceitfulness
of wealth choke it, making it unfruitful.
(Mat. 13:22)

The Trek:
Read Matthew 13:1-23

Nature Reflections:
What's the point of having a home by the lake without
having a porch overlooking it? That was the thought which
inspired us to add an enclosed porch to our home that, of
course, had a great view of the water. The day it was completed I rushed out to take in the spectacular view. What
I saw, instead, was weeds! There is a small strip of land
between our property line and the water's edge that had
become completely overgrown with brush, sumac trees and
other uninvited growth. Hence, our view of the lake was
cluttered and almost fully concealed. Not one to give up
easily, I got out my hand saw and some hedge trimmers,
and headed out to do battle with the weeds and ultimately
reclaimed my view of the lake. I then returned to my chair
on the porch and enjoyed a picture perfect view.

Our walk with God can be like my view from the porch. To grow in our faith we need to maintain a clear view of the Lord and keep our eyes steadily focused on him. Yet, so many times we find that the distractions of life creep in to clutter that view. Whether we are busy enjoying our pleasurable pastimes, or struggling with our problems and difficult situations, we find our attention has gradually been stolen away from the Lord. After a while we may suddenly discover we have completely lost sight of the one true source of peace and contentment. How appropriate that the Bible describes Jesus as the Living Water. It is by gazing upon him that we find all of our needs are truly met. So, whatever it takes, get out there and remove that clutter so that you, too, can reclaim the view. He's spectacular.

Nature Journal

49. Troubled Waters

But when he saw the wind, he was afraid and,
beginning to sink, cried out, "Lord, save me!"
(Mat 14:30)

The Trek:
Read Matthew 14:22-33

Nature Reflections:
The disciples got into a boat to take a journey they had made countless times before. They were well out on the lake when the storm hit them. They quickly realized they were in trouble. When they spotted a figure walking toward them on the thrashing waters, they cried out in utter terror. Then they heard a familiar voice saying, "Take courage! It is I. Don't be afraid." It was Jesus! Their fears subsided. But Peter wanted more. He cried, "Lord, if it's you, tell me to come to you on the water." Jesus invited him to come. Peter hopped out of the boat and began walking on the water toward Jesus. He would have made it if his attention not been diverted to the churning seas all around him. As soon as he looked away, he was no longer on top of the waves, but was quickly being overcome by them. Yet even in his panic, he still knew who to turn to. He cried, "Lord, save me!"

It is easy for us sideline commentators to see that Peter sank because he took his eyes off of his Savior and focused on the troubled waters. It is, perhaps, not quite so easy to objectively analyze our own responses when the storms of life threaten to drag us down. Is there really that much of a difference between Peter and us? The focus of Peter's saga, however, was not on his doubts but on Jesus' response. As soon as Peter cried for help we read, "Immediately Jesus reached out his hand and caught him." Just one cry to his Savior and Peter found himself safely sailing on a calm sea. Just one cry and the Savior will reach out his hand, in the same way, to you.

Nature Journal

50. Praying Up A Storm

*After leaving them, he went up
on a mountainside to pray.
(Mark 6:46)*

The Trek:
Read Mark 6:34-51

Nature Reflections:
The sun had long since set but I remained outside savoring
the peacefulness in the dark. I felt a sudden rush of wind
and literally within minutes the starry sky had completely
clouded over. The glassy water transformed into a crashing,
churning sea before my eyes. As the first drop of rain hit me,
I knew I had seconds to get inside if I were to avoid an unan-
ticipated evening shower. It was a typical sudden storm on
the River. Once inside I peered out the window and noticed
a small boat out on the water caught, no doubt, by surprise
in the sudden storm. As it moved slowly ahead in the pelt-
ing rain, its bow and stern lights appeared as wildly bounc-
ing balls in the darkness as the boat's hull violently pounded
against the oncoming waves. I said a silent prayer that it
would get home safely.

A similar kind of storm hit the disciples the night Jesus sent them out in the boat. They had already had an exhausting day when they found themselves in this full blown gale. Jesus had also had a demanding day. That is one reason he sent his disciples on ahead. While they were busy rowing, he was busy praying. He knew, better than anyone, the importance of spending time alone with the Father. As soon as he was finished, Jesus was recharged, refreshed, and ready to tackle even the forces of nature. After all, for the One who made the seas, walking on them was nothing! He walked atop the crashing waves to his struggling disciples in their time of need. He calmed their fears, and the raging seas. Jesus had prepared himself to calm the stormy seas with prayer. Prayer is how we, too, can handle the storms of life.

Nature Journal

51. Positive and Negative Forces

Photo courtesy NOAA

He replied, "I saw Satan fall like lightning from heaven." (Lk. 10:18)

The Trek:
Read Luke 10:1-24

Nature Reflections:
I was sitting on the dock overlooking calm waters. There wasn't as much as a breath of wind—then there was! With one massive gust it began. In less than a minute the still waters were covered with whitecaps and the sun was snuffed out by angry looking clouds. A flash of lightning exploded in the black sky followed by a deafening clap of thunder. I quickly decided to watch the rest of the storm from inside the house. Lightning is an electrical discharge that occurs between one cloud and another, or between a cloud and the earth. It can appear as a jagged streak (called forked lightning), a vast flash in the sky (sheet lightning) or as a brilliant ball (ball lightning). It is thought that temperature and water vapor pressure in clouds create the positive and negative ions that cause lightning. In 1752 Ben Franklin proved that lightning and electricity are identical.

The Bible states that "Satan himself masquerades as an angel of light" (2 Cor. 11:14). Light, of course, is a good thing, as is electricity. But anyone struck by a lightning bolt, who lives to describe it, will assure you it can also be very dangerous. Satan was created beautiful and powerful. But he used those positive attributes for evil. The deadly mix of positive and negative caused a heavenly reaction and he was cast from his position like a lightning bolt. Though Satan remains powerful for a time, Jesus assured his disciples, "I have given you authority . . . to overcome all the power of the enemy; nothing will harm you" (Lk. 10:19). So, next time you see a lightning bolt, go inside fast, but rejoice in knowing that "greater is he that is in you, than he that is in the world" (1 Jn 4:4).

Nature Journal

52. A Soft Touch

Photo courtesy Janet S. Robbins

If you then, though you are evil, know how to give good gifts to your children, how much more will your Father in heaven give the Holy Spirit to those who ask him!
(Lk. 11:13)

The Trek:
Read Luke 11:1-13

Nature Reflections:
Word must be out that my husband is a soft touch. Wild animals seem to somehow sense that he's good for a free handout. Bob was sitting in his car one day munching on French fries when he noticed an old, fat gray squirrel sitting directly below him on the ground. The squirrel was staring intently at him with a hungry Oliver Twist look on his little face. "You want a French fry, old man?" Bob asked as he tossed one to his newfound friend. Apparently that is exactly what the squirrel had in mind. He gobbled up the French fry and immediately peered up at Bob looking for more. Bob hadn't anticipated having to share his lunch but, like I said, he's a soft touch. So for the next few moments they dined together, man and squirrel, on Bob's French fries. When the last fry

was done, the squirrel clearly was not. Suddenly, he began to furiously wave his paw at Bob in a beckoning motion. Bob could almost imagine him yelling, "Come on!!! More fries, please!!" Whether it was the lack of fries, or Bob's peals of laughter, the squirrel finally decided to move on.

While we laugh at the tenacity of the old gray squirrel, God has told us to be just as bold in our approach to him. He has told us, "So I say to you: Ask and it will be given to you; seek and you will find; knock and the door will be opened to you. For everyone who asks receives; he who seeks finds; and to him who knocks, the door will be opened" (Lk. 11:9,10). You see, when it comes to meeting his children's needs, God is a soft touch. Just accept his invitation and you, too, can come and dine.

Nature Journal

53. Sneakers

Then he said, "This is what I'll do. I will tear down my barns and build bigger ones, and there I will store all my grain and my goods. And I'll say to myself, 'You have plenty of good things laid up for many years. Take life easy; eat, drink and be merry.'"

(Lk. 12:18-19)

The Trek:
Read Luke 12:15-34

Nature Reflections:
We keep a big bag of birdseed in our basement. Since we scoop what we need right out of the bag, we rarely need to lift it off the ground. So, I was surprised one day when I moved the bag and discovered, as seeds poured out all over the floor, that it had a hole in the bottom. After sweeping up the mess, I transferred all the seeds into a new, sturdier bag. A few weeks later I went down to refill the bird feeder and found that an even larger hole had clearly been gnawed through the bag. Apparently we were feeding more than just birds. We found a sealable container for our seeds after that. The next spring I started to slip on the old pair of sneakers I keep in the basement for gardening but didn't get too far. The entire

toe area of both shoes was filled with birdseed. Our bag thief had stored his stolen goods away for future use. He probably thought he was set for life. In the end, he lost it all.

The Bible describes a man who had amassed so much wealth that he had to build new barns to hoard it all away. Just when he thought he was set for life, he died. He, too, lost it all. Now, there is absolutely nothing wrong with acquiring earthly wealth (unless one uses someone else's sneaker to store it in). What does matter is where your heart is. The Scriptures encourage us to invest our energies into having "a treasure in heaven that will not be exhausted, where no thief comes near and no moth destroys. For where your treasure is, there your heart will be also" (Lk. 12:33-34). You might call that kind of treasure "seeds of faith."

Nature Journal

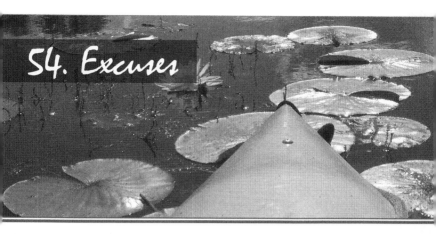

54. Excuses

But they all alike began to make excuses . . .
(Lk. 14:18)

The Trek:
Read Luke 14:1-24

Nature Reflections:
I almost decided against it. It was late, cool, too close to sunset, I was tired, and it would take a lot of extra effort. But as
I stood there debating, a quick glance out the window at the
beckoning waters made the decision for me. "I am going for
a boat ride!" I changed my clothes, dragged my kayak out
of the shed, fastened on my life jacket and in no time at all,
I was paddling toward the center of the lake. It was a calm
evening and the water was like glass. The brilliant fall colors
at the water's edge were being spotlighted by the setting sun
on the opposite horizon. "Magnificent!" When I reached the
middle of the lake I turned the boat around just in time to
watch a spectacular sunset, its colors blazing back to me in
stereo on the water's surface. I rowed back home in the ebbing twilight refreshed, inspired, and renewed. I had known all

along that, for me, it is always worth the effort to spend time by the water.

Later that evening, I thought about the struggle I had about doing something I knew I would benefit from. I was struck by how similar it was to a choice we believers make every day. We all realize that our primary source of inspiration and renewal comes from spending time with the Lord. Yet, it is so easy to make excuses—I'm too tired, it's too late, I have too much to do. However, a quick glance at our beckoning Savior's face should make the decision easy. He longs to spend time with us, and when we do, we will come to see his glory which far surpasses even the most magnificent sunset. In fact, the Son never sets!

Nature Journal

55. You Rock!

Some of the Pharisees in the crowd said to Jesus, "Teacher, rebuke your disciples!" "I tell you," he replied, "if they keep quiet, the stones will cry out."

(Lk 19:39, 40)

The Trek:

Read Luke 19:29-44

Nature Reflections:

When I was in High School I was an avid rock collector. I went to gem and mineral shows, traded specimens with friends, and even did some rock hunting of my own on occasion. My tastes were fairly eclectic ranging everywhere from precious gems, to fossils, to "just rocks" that I liked the looks of. My favorite, of course, is amethyst since it is my birth stone, and also because I love the color purple. I bought myself a big bag of assorted tumbled rocks that included such favorites as agate, obsidian and tiger's eye. I also loved the sparkly rocks like fool's gold (pyrite) and mica, and the crystals like quartz and feldspar. My uncle gave me a bag of stones he had collected that included speck-sized pieces of emeralds, garnets, opals, rubies and other precious gems (which, at that size and quality, were obviously not all that precious—but to me, they were priceless treasures). What amazed me was that under the single classification of "rock" one could find samples of virtually every shape and size, and every color of the rainbow.

When Jesus entered Jerusalem riding on a donkey, the religious leaders tried to shush the crowds who were singing, shouting, and worshiping him. He responded by telling them that even if the people stopped singing their praises, the stones would continue to do so. Some have suggested that Jesus was only speaking metaphorically when he made such a statement. But I think that anyone who has even superficially studied rocks and minerals could argue that these beautiful masterpieces already do give glory to God. Their rich diversity, color and beauty clearly cry out in praise of their Maker. But don't let that stop you from praising him. Just jump right in and join along.

Nature Journal

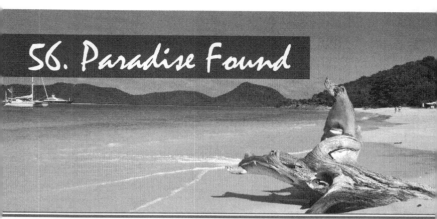

56. Paradise Found

Jesus answered him, "I tell you the truth, today you will be with me in paradise."
(Lk. 23:43)

The Trek:
Read Luke 23:33-46

Nature Reflections:

Paradise! The word itself evokes images of lush natural beauty and tranquility. It is a theme frequently found in stories, novels, and movies. Even Hollywood has been captivated with the concept of utopia as evidenced by such classic films as "Lost Horizons" and the discovery of an idyllic place called Shangri-la. There is a yearning in our hearts for such a place—a place where time stands blissfully still, where youthfulness is everlasting, and where peace and utter contentment reign eternal. Those who believe the Bible realize such a place truly did exist. The Garden of Eden was not a utopian fantasy but an actual place here on earth where humankind was created and first lived. Perhaps that is why there is something inside of us that longs to return to such a place. The word, "Eden" literally means pleasure or delight. It was a place untouched by sin, pollution, or even death. Then, through our own unfaithfulness to our loving Maker, we were permanently banned from the garden designed for our delight.

The Bible is not, however, a story about paradise lost. Quite the contrary. It assures us that God will one day restore this world to a place of eternal, sinless utopia. We are told, "But in keeping with his promise we are looking forward to a new heaven and a new earth, the home of righteousness" (2 Pet. 3:13). Those who spend their lives searching for utopia in this present world will end up disappointed. Those who pursue a relationship with the One who made it will one day hear words similar to those Jesus once uttered, ". . . today you will be with me in paradise." If you seek to find your delight in him you will go from paradise lost to Paradise found in Jesus.

Nature Journal

57. Hoover

Jesus said to them, "I tell you the truth, it is not Moses who has given you the bread from heaven, but it is my Father who gives you the true bread from heaven."

(John 6:32)

The Trek:
Read John 6:1-14, 26-32

Nature Reflections:
We named him Hoover because he eats like a vacuum cleaner. We first noticed the chipmunk eating seeds that had fallen from the bird feeder. Taking pity on the little fellow, Bob went out and set the feeder on the ground. We watched from the porch as the chipmunk discovered this great fortune that had befallen him. He jumped into the feeder, stuffed his cheeks with seeds, and happily bounded off. Bob went out and re-hung the feeder. He sat back down on the porch and realized that the chipmunk had followed him up the steps and was on his hind feet peering through the screen. The look on his fuzzy face could best be described by quoting Oliver Twist: "Please sir, might I have more?" At first I thought of Hoover as Bob's pet chipmunk but by the end of the summer it seemed more accurate to think of Bob as Hoover's pet human. Hoover needed only to jump up on

the picnic table and Bob would come running with seeds. Hoover vacuumed them up from Bob's hand as he affectionately stroked the little fellow with the other.

As I watched this little creature contentedly eating from Bob's hand I thought of our Heavenly Father ever reaching out to satisfy the desires of our heart. Like Hoover, we did nothing to earn God's favor. His love is unconditional and his grace is free for the asking. He knows our needs before we even ask and longs for us to call out to him so he might come to us and abundantly pour his love and grace upon us. One taste of his goodness and we, too, will be asking, "Please Sir, might I have more?" And the good news is that, indeed, when we ask, he'll come running.

Nature Journal

> *For the bread of God is he who comes down*
> *from heaven and gives life to the world.*
> *(John 6:33)*

The Trek:

Read John 6:33-51

Nature Reflections:

This past spring we discovered one major flaw in the man/
chipmunk relationship Bob had with Hoover. On our first
day back at camp we were delighted to find Hoover waiting
for us on the picnic table. And as before, Bob immediately
ran out with the seeds. He lovingly patted Hoover's little
head as the tiny creature hungrily packed an entire handful
of seeds into his bulging cheeks. As he ran off to empty his
first load, we noticed he headed in a different direction than
the year before. Bob followed him and was horrified to discover Hoover had, indeed, found himself a new home—the
neighbors' garage! The neighbors would not be pleased about
a chipmunk storing seeds in their garage. But how does one
tell a chipmunk he had picked a very unsafe location for a
home. From Hoover's perspective he probably thought he
had discovered a mansion. In reality he had made a decision
that could ultimately prove fatal.

Unfortunately for Hoover, as much as Bob wanted to sit down and have a heart-to-heart, man-to-chipmunk talk with him, Bob did not speak chipmunk. Nor, did Hoover speak "bob." Bob could not communicate with his little friend to warn him of the dangers of living in the garage of someone not as fond of chipmunks as he was. Thankfully for us, that is where the comparison between Bob and God departs. God saw that we, too, had made some bad decisions that would ultimately prove fatal. But God was able to do what Bob could not. He came down, in the flesh, to deliver his message of hope and salvation. In fact, God actually became one of us, fully human yet fully God, not to merely point us in the right direction but to provide the way home.

Nature Journal

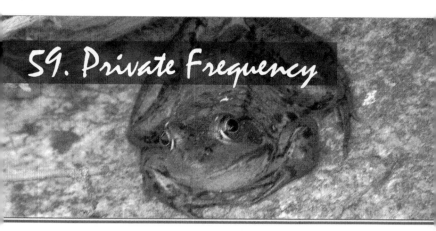

59. Private Frequency

> *When he has brought out all his own,*
> *he goes on ahead of them, and his sheep*
> *follow him because they know his voice.*
> *(John 10:4)*

The Trek:
Read John 10:1-16

Nature Reflections:

We almost had to cover our ears. The sound level was nearly deafening. No, we hadn't gone to a Three Dog Night concert although their hit song, "Jeremiah Was a Bullfrog" would have been quite appropriate. It was a warm spring evening and we had walked over to the bay to listen to the season's opener of the young tadpoles-turned-frog, or peepers as I've always called them. It is only the males that croak and they do so, quite enthusiastically, to attract females. Frogs vocalize by squeezing their lungs, with their nostrils and mouth shut. Many have vocal pouches that inflate like balloons and serve as a resonating chamber that enables them to sing with amazing volume for their size. The great variance in frog sounds is based on age, size and species. The young peepers make an extremely high pitched "peeping" noise which deepens as the summer progresses. The pitch or frequency changes in direct proportion to a frog's size. Some frogs call at a private frequency not used by other frogs. Frogs are also able to hear certain frequencies very clearly so that they hear their mates over the calls of other frogs.

God uses a method of communicating with us humans similar to that of the frogs. Jesus told his disciples that his followers would know his voice. Even amid the din of voices calling for our attention, beckoning us to follow them, the voice of our Savior comes through loud and clear. He has promised that all who truly seek him will find him. And to all who are sincerely listening for it, his voice will stand out from all the others. We will hear and know our Master's voice because we will hear him speaking directly to us on our own private frequency.

Nature Journal

60. Lazarus, Come Forth!

Photo courtesy USFWS

*Jesus said to her, "I am the resurrection and the life.
He who believes in me will live, even though he dies."*
(John 11:25)

The Trek:
Read John 11:20-44

Nature Reflections:
I kept my pet box turtle, Beasley, in a plastic tub in the house
but would often take him outside and set him on the lawn to
play with me. I knew I needed to watch him, of course, since
box turtles are prone to wandering off. However, I also knew
that they couldn't do it very fast. One day, Beasley and I were
playing on the lawn when the phone rang. Literally less than
a minute later I returned to find my beloved pet was gone!
I cried hysterically and my parents came running and we all
began to search the area. Then, my dad made a gruesome
discovery. One of the neighborhood dogs had found Beasley
and had chewed him into a bloody mess. My dad wrapped
the remains in newspaper and put him gently in the trash can
as I cried my little heart out. Later that night, dad went to
throw out some trash and there, sitting on top the pile, was

Beasley. He was probably more confused about his trash can ordeal than the dog's attack. Mom picked up my wounded pet, cared for his wounds, and even prayed over him. In no time at all, my pet was almost as good as new though he was strictly a house turtle after that.

While Beasley's adventures appeared to border on the miraculous, they can't compare to the adventures of Jesus' dear friend, Lazarus. There was no question about it. Lazarus was dead and had spent four days wrapped, not in newspapers, but grave clothes. But when Jesus gave the word, the dead man came out, resurrected—alive! Yes, this was a true miracle. Yet, no more miraculous than the new and eternal life he promises to everyone who puts their trust in him.

Nature Journal

61. Declaring the Wonders

Photo courtesy USFWS

When they heard this sound, a crowd came together in bewilderment, because each one heard them speaking in his own language.
(Acts 2:6)

The Trek:

Read Acts 2:1-6 and 38-47

Nature Reflections:

I was out for a morning walk when I heard a robin begin to sing. Or, was it? The bird had barely finished its song when the tune changed to that of a redwing blackbird. Next, the bird burst into a perfect rendition of a wren! I quickly realized I was enjoying my own private concert of a mockingbird. The scientific name for the mockingbird is *Mimus Polyglottos* which translates to "many-tongued mimic." Mockingbirds can perform anywhere from 25 to 30 songs, with some having produced up to 39 different bird species. Talk about being multi-lingual. As I listened, this little many-tongued mimic brought a scene from the Bible to mind. The Lord had told his disciples he would be sending them his Holy Spirit. As they gathered to celebrate Pentecost, the Holy Spirit came as promised. Tongues of fire appeared on each disciple and they began to speak in other languages. People who were visiting from all over the world were suddenly hearing their own language being spoken by these native Galileans. And what were they hearing? They exclaimed, "We hear them declaring the wonders of God in our own tongues!" (Acts 2:7).

I was amazed by the mockingbird's ability to so perfectly mimic other birds and creatures. Like the faithful believers at Pentecost, he was doing exactly what his Creator designed him to do. And in so doing, the mockingbird was declaring the wonders of God in his own unique way. Now, if God could use a wild bird to so gloriously testify of the wonders of his Creator, just think what he can do with each of us. When we speak, filled with his Holy Spirit, prompted by his love within us, others will be able to hear us declaring the wonders of God, and believe.

Nature Journal

62. When the Heat's On

About midnight Paul and Silas were praying and singing hymns to God, and the other prisoners were listening to them.
(Acts 16:25)

The Trek:
Read Acts 16:16-34

Nature Reflections:

I sat on the back porch with my eyes closed soaking in the sweet panoramic sounds of this warm summer's eve. Just after sunset the night air came alive with the joyful songs of the crickets. The cricket's ability to produce such a vast array of tones and rhythms is not from vocal cords but rather by rubbing its wings together. Only the male cricket has this ability which he uses to attract females and to drive off other males intruding on his territory. Because the song of crickets slows down as the temperature drops, one can roughly estimate the temperature by counting the number of chirps. The temperature in Fahrenheit degrees is determined by dividing the number of chirps per minute by four and adding 40. That is why, when the warmth of summer gives way to the cooler fall evenings, the cricket songs slowly wind down until they finally fade away altogether for the season.

Yes, you can measure the temperature by the song of the cricket. That's actually not such a bad idea for us humans. When the pressure is on, and the heat is turned up, those are the times we need to be reminded of God's presence more than ever. Paul and Silas were well aware of the importance of focusing on the Lord in times of trial. After being falsely accused, beaten, and thrown in prison, they could have started feeling sorry for themselves or blamed God for their difficulties. Instead, they had a praise concert. And once they started singing, you might say the jailhouse rocked! God caused an earthquake and set his worshiping saints free. Remember that next time you hear the crickets singing on a warm summer's night. Songs of praise always make a difference when the heat's on.

Nature Journal

63. Super-Natural

For since the creation of the world God's invisible qualities—his eternal power and divine nature—have been clearly seen, being understood from what has been made, so that men are without excuse.

(Romans 1:20)

The Trek:
Read Romans 1:1-20

Nature Reflections:

My love for nature has had an influence on the music I write. One of my earliest CDs was an entire album combining songs about nature with actual nature sounds such as birds, crickets, or loons. I called that CD "Only Natural" because, as the title song puts it, "it's only natural to believe in the Creator when I see how all creation testifies, through its marvelous design and endless beauty . . . A Master Designer." When I experience the wonder of God's creation—his sunsets, a loon's cry, a rose, or a lily—it is only natural for me to find my heart elevated in praise and worship. But, thinking about it, is that really a natural response? The dictionary defines "nature/natural" in several different ways including, "The world of living things and the outdoors", "the processes that produce and control the material world", "a creative and controlling force in the universe" or, "the ordinary course of nature: not marvelous or supernatural." On the other hand, "Supernatural" is defined as "that which is beyond nature, or what cannot be explained by the laws of the natural world" or "attributed to a power that transcends the laws of nature."

If one's definition of "natural" takes into account our having been created to respond to it then, yes, it is only natural to be awed by God's natural world. If all of nature is the work of God's hands, and if even my ability to experience it is a gift from him, then it is, by definition, "supernatural." In some ways, in a world where all things were created, including those creatures who have the ability to enjoy it, the two terms are almost synonymous. But either way you look at it, God's world and the praises of his people are supernatural.

Nature Journal

64. The Remnant

So too, at the present time there is a remnant chosen by grace (Rm. 11:5)

The Trek:
Read Romans 11:1-29

Nature Reflections:
It is a glorious day! Especially considering it is now late November. The puffy white clouds are slowly meandering through a brilliant blue sky over the sparkling waters of the lake. It is, however, noticeably different from a few months ago. There is a quietness completely unlike the summertime. There are no speedboats buzzing by—no clamor at the beach. The migratory birds have most likely already arrived at their southern destinations by now. Still, as I sit here enjoying the serenity and warmth, I am not alone. A lone fisherman stands on the opposite shore as a seagull soars overhead. A blue jay is squawking in the distance and our finches are contentedly eating at their feeder. And, of course, my beloved Bob is here with me, as well. Yes, there is a small remnant of us who'll be sticking around all year—a remnant who are able to enjoy this lovely day and others yet to come.

When I think of remnants, God's faithfulness always comes to mind. Remnants are the remains, or, those who remain. God knew from the beginning that mankind would not remain faithful to him. Yet, he promised he would remain faithful to mankind, and there would always be a remnant who remained faithful to him. Sometimes it seems like so few people love the Lord that all the believers must have migrated for the winter. As I sit here today and observe all the life still going on around me, and feel the warmth of the sun above me, I remember, once again, God's promise for all who remain faithful to him: "In that day the LORD Almighty will be a glorious crown, a beautiful wreath for the remnant of his people" (Is 28:5). It will, indeed, be a glorious day.

Nature Journal

65. Bad Press

You, then, why do you judge your brother? Or why do you look down on your brother? For we will all stand before God's judgment seat. . . .Therefore let us stop passing judgment on one another.
(Rm 14:10, 13)

The Trek:
Read Romans 14:1-19

Nature Reflections:
"Oh look honey, it's a loon!" Bob grabbed the camera as the low riding bird swam our way. After a few moments Bob responded, "No, it's just a cormorant." We both sighed in disappointment as Bob put the camera away. One would wonder why two such similar looking aquatic birds would elicit such entirely different reactions. It is due in part to the overpopulation problems currently facing cormorants. Back in the 1970s cormorants were put on a protected species list. Today, the cormorant population is at an all-time high. Add to that the fact that they are insatiable fish eaters and have cost the aquaculture industry millions of dollars, not to mention the loss to recreational fisherman. Their nicknames don't help much, either. The cormorant (Latin for "sea

crow") also has such flattering names as water turkey, water buzzard, and crow-duck. There is no doubt about it—the cormorant has had a lot of bad press.

In reality, cormorants play an important role in the environment. They are regulators of nature's complex food system by keeping fish from overpopulating. They are also an important environmental indicator species meaning that when cormorants are thriving, the environment is thriving. God designed the cormorant with a special purpose and function in his natural world. It's amazing what a little bad press can do to one of his creatures. And that is exactly what we do when we gossip, criticize, backbite, and spread rumors about each other. Hurtful words not only have a devastating effect on others but are an insult to their Creator. God uniquely designed every one of us with a very special pur-pose and function. If we choose to ignore the bad press we will soon discover beauty in every living thing and in every precious person he made.

Nature Journal

66. Tunnel Vision

*If the whole body were an eye, where would the
sense of hearing be? If the whole body were
an ear, where would the sense of smell be?
(1 Cor. 12:17)*

The Trek:
Read 1 Cor. 12:1-18

Nature Reflections:

Now, I don't want to point any fingers but . . . somebody ate
my tulip bulbs! I had planted several in containers and placed
them under the porch for the winter. When spring finally
arrived I had anticipated a glorious display of color. I got
nothing! When I dug up the containers there were no bulbs
to be found. Now, unless they were beamed up by space
aliens, one could only conclude someone stole them. Later
that evening, I spotted a little brown mole scurrying under
the porch and knew I'd spotted my thief. Moles are known
for having bad eyesight and messing up lawns with their endless tunneling. They are seldom seen above ground, crawling
somewhat awkwardly on their knuckles. However, there is no
need to pity the little guys. What they lack in vision and agil-
ity above ground, they more than compensate for with their
underground digging skills and other heightened senses. The

mole's nose and tail have vibration sensors so highly tuned they can actually hear earthworms and grubs chewing. Then, with their expert digging skills they can effortlessly tunnel themselves to dinner.

We can learn a valuable lesson from Mr. Mole. Rather than dwelling on our weaknesses, and what we *can't* do, we should use tunnel vision and focus on the strengths God has given us. Like the little mole, you too have been perfectly designed for the life God has given you. As you use the gifts he has given you, you will find yourself moving through life and bearing fruit almost effortlessly. By the way, did you know that the mole eats about 60 lbs. of grubs per year? That many grubs could destroy an entire lawn. Maybe Mr. Mole isn't so bad, after all. And I really don't know *who* stole my tulip bulbs.

Nature Journal

67. Comfort

Praise be to the God and Father of our Lord Jesus Christ, the Father of compassion and the God of all comfort, who comforts us in all our troubles, so that we can comfort those in any trouble with the comfort we ourselves have received from God.
(2 Cor. 1:3, 4)

The Trek:
Read 2 Corinthians 1:1-14

Nature Reflections:
We are called to comfort one another with Christ's love. I admit that, at times, it would be much easier just to disappear into the woods and not deal with anyone's problems. Thankfully, this is not how God dealt with me in my time of need. There was a time in my life when I was physically, emotionally, and spiritually broken. Frankly, I wanted to die. God had a much different plan for me. In fact, it was there at my lowest point that he accomplished his greatest work in my life. He showed me that even when I had completely given up on myself, he never gave up on me. Slowly but surely, he led me out of the darkness and into his glorious light. When I opened his word it was as if every page was

133

speaking just to me. Similarly, when I sat at the end of the dock, or took a walk in the woods, the wonder of his natural world spoke directly to my heart and assured me of his perfect plan for my life.

Today, I realize that dark period was one of the best times of my life. No, not pleasant, by any means, but it transformed me from being a spiritual infant, into someone God could use to reach out to others. He allowed me to go through the darkness so that I could one day help others find their way out, too. I still like to disappear into the woods, not to run away from problems, but to spend time with my Creator and Savior. Now, when I see someone struggling or in pain, I long to reach out and offer them the comfort I, myself, received from God. Perhaps we could go, together, for a walk in the woods!

Nature Journal

68. No Place Like Home

We are confident, I say, and would prefer to be away
from the body and at home with the Lord. So
we make it our goal to please him, whether we are
at home in the body or away from it.
(2 Cor. 5:8, 9)

The Trek:
Read 2 Corinthians 5:1-17

Nature Reflections:
We knew wrens liked to build their nests in unique places.
But we were still surprised when we discovered our boat hoist
had become someone's home. Our little boat is held out of
the water by two hoists built into the dock. The metal hoists
are hollow and have a small hole at the very top that perfectly
suited one of the wrens. As I unknowingly began to turn the
crank one day, Mrs. Wren darted past me and began to scold
me furiously before disappearing into the now stick-filled
hole. Apparently, our infrequent boat rides weren't enough to
force an eviction. Within the week, our boat hoist started to
peep, and both Mr. and Mrs. Wren began the unending task
of feeding the newly hatched chicks. Wrens are chubby little
birds with short tails. What they lack in their drab coloring is

made up for by their exquisite melodious songs. They are perhaps best known for their equal opportunity nesting habits. Wrens will nest almost anywhere including boots, car radiators, mailboxes, clotheslines, and, of course, boat hoists.

God designed wrens with an instinct to nest in all kinds of unique places. They're not fussy. They'll strategically place a few twigs and consider virtually anywhere home. Perhaps we humans can learn from the wrens. We spend a lot of time, energy and money on our earthly homes as if we would be living in them forever. But as Paul reminds us, our permanent home yet awaits us. If our greatest desire in this life is to please him, we'll find we are less concerned about the kind of home we briefly dwell in, in this life. By the way, there is a vacancy in our second boat hoist. Not a lot of extra space but the view is marvelous.

Nature Journal

66. Zapped!

*And no wonder, for Satan himself
masquerades as an angel of light.*
(2 Cor. 11:14)

The Trek:
Read 2 Corinthians 11:1-15

Nature Reflections:
I hate bees. I mean, I really hate bees! So, I was not pleased to discover a yellow jacket nest in the siding of our house one day. My heroic husband went out to do battle. He sprayed the siding with insecticide, and completely sealed the hole where they had been getting in. We thought the crisis was over until we went downstairs later that day and discovered the entire nest of angry bees, unable to exit elsewhere, had poured into the basement. Suddenly, the person who loathes bees so much had thousands of them swarming inside her house. My first thought was to call a Realtor. Bob, however, was undaunted. After quickly realizing insecticide was both ineffective and dangerous, he had another idea. He got out our electric bug zapper, hung it up in the middle of the basement and turned out all the other lights. Sure enough, it worked. Over the

next few days it sounded a bit like a popcorn popper down there, but ultimately, in the battle of Bob versus the bees, Bob claimed the victory.

The zapper worked because the bees, desperate to find their way to freedom, came to the light. Instead of freedom, however, they were led to their own destruction. How appropriate that the Bible refers to Satan as an angel of light. He, too, tries to lure us away from the true Light, and those who take the bait will be led to their own destruction. Yes, we need to be aware of Satan's tactics and not be led astray even by things that appear good. But more importantly, we must come to truly know the real thing. When our eyes are focused on the Light of the World, the light of the imposter will be dim in comparison.

Nature Journal

70. Something to Crow About

That is why, for Christ's sake, I delight in weaknesses, in insults, in hardships, in persecutions, in difficulties. For when I am weak, then I am strong.
(2 Cor 12:10)

The Trek:
Read 2 Corinthians 12:1-10

Nature Reflections:

I'd always thought of them as nuisance birds but my mother-in-law considers them pets. All Mom Mondore has to do is walk out the back door and her crows flock to her. It no doubt helps that she often feeds them bread crumbs. The crow is a large, glossy black bird that is found almost world-wide. While crows don't sing, they have over 20 different calls to communicate with. Crows eat a wide variety of food ranging from seeds to dead animals. They are also known for nest plundering and for destroying eggs and nestlings of other birds. A group of crows is called a "murder" of crows, based in part on a legend that crows form tribunals to judge and punish the bad behavior of a member of the flock. If the verdict goes against the defendant, that bird is murdered by the flock. While this is only a folk tale, it is true that crows will kill a dying crow who doesn't belong in their territory, or to weed out the weak and feeble.

Thankfully, God doesn't judge us using the system employed by crows. As he put it himself, "On the contrary, those parts of the body that seem to be weaker are indispensable, and the parts that we think are less honorable we treat with special honor" (1 Cor. 12:22, 23). In the same way, "We who are strong ought to bear with the failings of the weak and not to please ourselves" (Rm 15:1). To God, our weaknesses are potentially our greatest strengths. The Apostle Paul learned firsthand that God's grace was not only sufficient for his weaknesses, but that they became the vehicle through which his power flows. No wonder Paul came to realize his weaknesses were actually something to crow about.

Nature Journal

Photo courtesy ForestWander.com

> *In him we have redemption through his*
> *blood, the forgiveness of sins, in accordance*
> *with the riches of God's grace.*
> *(Eph 1:7)*

The Trek:
Read Ephesians 1:1-14

Nature Reflections:
It was a brisk winter day and I was out for a chilly morning run. While the exercise was refreshing and invigorating, the scenery had much to be desired. In fact, the deadness of this particularly gloomy December day reminded me of watching an old, colorless black and white movie. Suddenly, I heard a familiar song and looked up to discover a brilliant red cardinal sitting in a nearby tree. The cardinal is one of the most popular and distinctive backyard birds in North America with its bright red color and crested head. Unlike most songbirds the cardinal doesn't migrate so its lovely tune and bold colors can be enjoyed throughout year. Cardinals are among the few bird species that mate for life and remain together year round so if you see one at the feeder you'll usually also see its partner.

The brilliant red color and cheery song I enjoyed that day brought brightness and life to the otherwise dead and dreary winter scene. Perhaps that is why cardinals are so often pictured on Christmas cards. Jesus came to earth and, as Isaiah wrote, "The people walking in darkness have seen a great light; on those living in the land of the shadow of death a light has dawned" (Is. 9:2). He brought light and life to a dark and dying world. His arrival was a stark contrast replacing despair with hope, and death with life. I once heard the question posed, "What color is forgiveness?" It is red because our sins are forgiven when they are covered by the blood of Christ. So, next time you see a cardinal think of "him who loves us and has freed us from our sins by his blood" (Rev 1:5) and remember that the color of forgiveness is red.

Nature Journal

72. The Upside-Down Bird

Photo courtesy USDA

I know what it is to be in need, and I know what it is to have plenty. I have learned the secret of being content in any and every situation, whether well fed or hungry, whether living in plenty or in want.
(Phil 4:12)

The Trek:
Read Philippians 4:1-12

Nature Reflections:

"Honey, look! There's a bird walking upside down on the tree branch," I exclaimed to Bob after my first encounter with a nuthatch. We quickly discovered that watching these highly animated, gravity defying little birds was like watching cartoon characters at the movies. Never creatures to wear out a welcome, they zip in, grab a single seed, then dart over to a nearby branch to eat it. But unlike other birds who hold seeds with their feet and crack them open with their bills, the nuthatches will jam them into a crack and then "hatch" them with their bills. But the most fascinating attribute of these vaudevillian acrobats is their unique ability to walk down a tree headfirst. They can also hang upside down from a horizontal branch seemingly just as easy as if they were on top of it. This ability has earned them their nickname, the "upside-down bird."

The Apostle Paul seemed to have some of the same attributes as the nimble nuthatch. He never stopped moving around as he traveled the globe with the message of salvation. But even more importantly, he had an amazing ability to "walk upside-down." Whether he was visiting kings, or sitting in prison, Paul continued to press on. Regardless of the situation he was in, Paul had learned the secret of being content, and even victorious. As he put it, "I can do everything through him who gives me strength" (Phil. 4:12). You might say he had learned to defy gravity. Paul had been freed from the things of this earth that drag us down and defeat us. And the source of Paul's strength is available to every believer. We can defy the gravity pulling us down in this life, just like the upside-down bird, when we walk together with Jesus.

Nature Journal

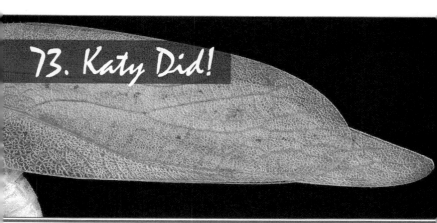

73. Katy Did!

*I can do everything through
him who gives me strength.
(Phil. 4:13)*

The Trek:
Read Philippians 4:13-18 and Romans 8:33-39

Nature Reflections:
Sometimes, on a warm summer night after working late Bob will walk in the door and greet me with, "Did did did! Did did did!" We'll both giggle and then go back outside for a few minutes to listen to the concert being performed by the later summer Katydids. Katydids are members of the Orthoptera family which is one of the noisiest of all insect varieties. Like their cousins, the grasshoppers, they produce their sounds by rubbing body parts together. They were named after the sound they make, "ka-tee-did." Katydids are tree-living insects that are usually only heard after dark from late summer through early fall. They are about 2 ½ inches long and have wings that look like green leaves. On hot summer nights their "did did dids" are fast and continuous. As the nights get cooler, they go into a lower gear as if they are winding down for the season. Still, whether fast or slow, hot or cold, it is the

same sweet song. No matter how dark or cold the night, they will keep singing right up until the first frost.

I have often playfully thought about how Katydids never sing, "Katy didn't." No, Katys always did! And that would actually make a great theme song for us believers. We have been assured that we can do all things when we have the power of God at work in our lives. Whatever each day brings, when we face it together with him we have the confidence that "in all these things we are more than conquerors through him who loved us" (Rm. 8:37). That means we will be able to look back some day and realize that no matter how dark the night we "did did did" it all "through him who gives me strength."

Nature Journal

74. A Bird in the Hand

But my God shall supply all your need according
to his riches in glory by Christ Jesus.
(Phil 4:19)

The Trek:
Read Philippians 4:19-23 and Luke 12:1-7

Nature Reflections:
I clearly remember what inspired me to try. It was the picture
on a church bulletin. A perky little chickadee was sitting in
the palm of an outstretched hand full of sunflower seeds.
The caption read, "But my God shall supply all your need
according to his riches in glory by Christ Jesus." I had never
seen a wild bird eat out of someone's hand and the idea
enthralled me. I soon discovered it is easy to train chickadees
to eat from one's hand—from *my* hand. All it took was a
little patience, some sunflower seeds and I made several new
chick-friends who now dine with me regularly.

As I watched the little birds landing so trustingly on
my hand, one of Jesus' illustrations came to mind. The
chickadees had found what they considered to be a safe and
bountiful source of food. At the same time, it brought me

great delight to be their provider. Jesus told us to "Look at the birds of the air; they do not sow or reap or store away in barns, and yet your heavenly Father feeds them. Are you not much more valuable than they?" (Mat. 6:26). God has been feeding the wild birds since the day he created them. He cares about every one of his creatures regardless of how small or seemingly insignificant it may be. If he cares that much about wild birds just think how much he cares about each of us. God has extended his hand to everyone—to you—offering his love and his provision, and it gives him great delight to do so. Like that little chickadee we need only step out in faith and "Taste and see that the LORD is good . . . those who seek the LORD lack no good thing" (Ps. 34:8, 10).

Nature Journal

75. Loon Magic

For by him all things were created: things in heaven and on earth, visible and invisible, whether thrones or powers or rulers or authorities; all things were created by him and for him.

(Col 1:16)

The Trek:

Read Colossians 1:1-17

Nature Reflections:

I have never cared for the expression "crazy as a loon." And not just because it's been used on me. It is an insult to this creature of such wonder and beauty. A quick scan of any nature shop will reveal how popular the loon (Gavia immer) is. It has been painted by artists, recorded by musicians, carved by wildlife sculptors and written about by naturalists. The call of the loon has captivated the hearts of nature lovers perhaps more than any other creature. One can purchase numerous recordings of loons with titles such as "Loon Magic" and "The Mystical Call of the Loon." While the loon is perhaps best known for its wails, it actually has four different types of calls which include wails, tremolos, yodels and hoots. The tremolos or "laugh" of the loon is what earned it the "crazy as a loon" expression.

The most fascinating call is the yodel which is produced only by the male. This call is so unique that each individual male can be identified by its own personal vocal signature encoded in its yodel. That makes some of those album titles more appropriate than their authors may have even realized. The dictionary describes "Magic" as 1) the use of means believed to have supernatural power over natural forces, or 2) an extraordinary power or influence seemingly from a supernatural source. "Mystical" is defined as 1) having a spiritual meaning or reality that is neither apparent to the senses nor obvious to the intelligence, or 2) an individual's direct subjective communion with God. Yes, this amazing creature, with its enchanting calls and unique vocal signatures, truly points to the "magic" of an extraordinary Creator. He is the God who not only knows each of us personally but who responds when we call.

Nature Journal

76. The Architect

And he is the head of the body, the church; he is the beginning and the firstborn from among the dead, so that in everything he might have the supremacy.
(Col. 1:18)

The Trek:
Read Colossians 1:18-29

Nature Reflections:

The story made the news all over the world. A small child fell into a gorilla cage at a zoo. The terrified and wounded child screamed as the crowd looked on in helpless horror. Surely, he would be torn apart. Then, the seemingly impossible occurred. A female gorilla picked up the wounded child protecting him from the other gorillas, and eventually carried him to safety. One article that was written by an anthropologist pointed out that this kind of maternal instinct from gorilla to human should not surprise us since gorilla genes are almost identical to human genes. There is, indeed, an incredible similarity between the DNA of apes and humans. For that matter, there are almost as many similarities between the genes of mice and men (though it would be hard to imagine a mother mouse being quite as accommodating should one of us fall into her nest). Nevertheless, scientists have found that DNA remains consistently similar and consistently complex in every living thing on the earth. But then, such similarities really shouldn't surprise us since the genes of gorillas, mice, and men were all designed by the same Creator.

The Bible teaches that by Jesus "all things were created . . . He is before all things, and in him all things hold together . . . after he is the *beginning* . . ."(Col 1:16-18). The Greek word used in this passage for "beginning" is "arche." The concordance defines arche as a commencement, chief, beginning, magistrate, power, or principality. Arche is also the word we derive "Architect" from. How appropriate. Jesus is the Chief Architect of all creation. Through him the world and every living thing in it had a commencement or beginning. The similarities found in the genes of every creature reveal the identifiable architectural style of their common Originator, the Divine Arche!

Nature Journal

77. Blowdown

For every house is built by someone,
but God is the builder of everything.
(Heb. 3:4)

The Trek:
Read Hebrews 3:1-14

Nature Reflections:

On September 11, 2001 America experienced one of the most vicious attacks in its history when two hijacked passenger jets were intentionally crashed into the World Trade Center. A few days later, a naturalist spoke at our institution and shared his thoughts on the event. He showed a picture of a blowdown he had taken. This natural catastrophe had destroyed acres of land and flattened an entire forest. He told the spellbound audience that within six years one could not even tell that the blowdown had occurred. In time, even the forest would grow back. Nature, he explained, will restore itself. His point was that, in time, we too would recover from this tragedy. Though his words sounded inspiring, something was noticeably lacking from his message. Yes, nature was designed to replenish itself. But what caused the catastrophe on 9/11 wasn't natural. Nor is the hope that can be found in such tragic situations.

153

I thought of all the families whose loved ones would never be coming home. Buildings can be rebuilt but human lives cannot be replaced. And replacing fallen structures does not deal with the ongoing problem of evil. A purely naturalistic response offers no explanation, no real healing, no hope. The only true comfort to be found in tragedies such as this is in the assurance of a good and sovereign God, and the hope of a life beyond this one. In nature, catastrophic events such as blowdowns are all part of the circle of life. God designed the natural world to continually restore and replace itself. He had something much better in mind for mankind. By offering us a personal relationship with himself, he has provided us with hope amidst the blowdowns of this life, and the assurance that we'll spend eternity with him.

Nature Journal

78. Aggressive

Photo courtesy Dick Daniels

*Let us therefore come boldly unto the throne
of grace, that we may obtain mercy,
and find grace to help in time of need.
(Heb. 4:16 KJV)*

The Trek:
Read Hebrews 4

Nature Reflections:
I cut the giant sunflower and wired it to the top of our bird feeder. I no sooner got back in the house when the action began. With raucous squawks and a flurry of wings, the blue jay descended upon the feeder and began systematically dismantling the sunflower one seed at a time. From my vantage point at the window, I was able to sit face to face with this magnificent, blue and white bird. After watching finches he looked gigantic and, speaking of finches, one look at this feisty intruder and the entire bunch had abandoned the feeder. I remember hearing someone once say they didn't like blue jays because they are such aggressive birds. "Bullies" she called them. As I watched the triumphant lone diner I could see her point.

We have all known someone we would consider too aggressive. But being bold and assertive doesn't necessarily have to be a negative trait. The Scriptures encourage us to be bold in sharing our faith. However, this boldness is not attained through our own strength but through God working within us. We read, "And they were all filled with the Holy Spirit and spoke the word of God boldly" (Acts 4:31). So in order to receive this gift we must also be aggressive in seeking God. He has invited us to approach him with confidence so we can receive all of the promises he made to those he calls his own. Yes, being too aggressive can be bad, but when used appropriately it is a strength. The blue jay may not have attracted a lot of finches but he sure enjoyed his sunflower. When we boldly approach our Heavenly Father we will discover he loves to pour his blessings on all who come to him and ask.

Nature Journal

79. An Uphill Climb

You need to persevere so that when you have done the will of God, you will receive what he has promised.
(Heb. 10:36)

The Trek:
Read Hebrews 10:19-39

Nature Reflections:
Bob and I discovered a big turtle sitting at the top of our driveway and thought we were doing him a favor when we carried him all the way back down the hill and set him near the bay. We later realized it was neither a favor, nor a "him." The next day, *Mrs.* Turtle made the long journey back up the hill in a renewed attempt to lay her eggs. Apparently, once she set her mind to it, not even well-intended, uninformed humans could deter her from her goal. Despite the setback, Mrs. Turtle found her way back to the very same spot and we watched from a distance as she went about her business. She dug a hole in the sandy ground, deposited her eggs, gently covered the hole then slowly made her way back to the bay, mission accomplished (probably muttering to herself, "thank goodness those bothersome people didn't interfere this time!").

My heart goes out to that persistent mother turtle who, two times in a row, made a long, hard trip carrying a very heavy load, to accomplish her goal. I think we can all relate to her making that difficult trek up the hill, only to find herself right back where she started. Life can be that way at times. However, God can use those frustrating events in our lives for our good if we let him. He tells us, "Blessed is the man who perseveres under trial, because when he has stood the test, he will receive the crown of life that God has promised to those who love him" (Jms. 1:12). So, next time you find yourself in a difficult uphill climb, don't look back. Press on, remembering that "I can do everything through him who gives me strength" (Phil 4:13).

Nature Journal

80. Things Unseen

By faith we understand that the universe was formed at God's command, so that what is seen was not made out of what was visible.

Heb. 11:3

The Trek:

Read Hebrews 11:1-16

Nature Reflections:

It has always been easy for me to believe that God created the Universe and everything in it. My simple faith was partly from growing up in a Christian home. But I also believe God, himself, helped me see this so clearly even as a young, nature-loving child. I knew that all that I loved was the work of his hands. John Dalton, the founder of the atomic theory, had that same kind of simple faith. His faith was key to his scientific accomplishments. Because he was willing to believe in the existence of things beyond his own limited perception, he eventually applied that principle to his studies of the atom. In 1803 Dalton, a devout God-fearing Quaker, presented what has become known as the modern atomic theory. Atomism is the study of atoms and the forces which hold them together. Despite its inaccuracies, the core concepts of Dalton's atomic theory have remained foundations of modern physical science.

The Scriptures give evidence for the existence of unseen things. Perhaps that, in part, is what motivated Dalton to seek out and discover all that he did about the atom. We read, "Now faith is being . . . certain of what we do not see . . . what is seen was not made out of what was visible" (Heb. 11:1, 3). The Apostle Paul wrote, "For by him all things were created: things in heaven and on earth, visible and invisible . . . and in him all things hold together" (Col 1:16,17). There is comfort to be found in knowing that the One who put all those atoms together to form the world, is still actively involved in keeping them in place. Surely, the God who holds the entire Universe together can be trusted to uphold each of us in every situation we face in our daily lives.

Nature Journal

81. The Sky Pilots

Instead, they were longing for a better country—a heavenly one. Therefore God is not ashamed to be called their God, for he has prepared a city for them.
(Heb. 11:16)

The Trek:
Read Hebrews 11:13-40

Nature Reflections:
They were called the "sky pilots" by the old-time lumberjacks they traveled through the forests to visit. The first person to earn the title was Frank Higgins, a preacher from Minnesota. In 1895, Higgins went to visit the Kettle River logging camp and was asked by one of the lumberjacks, "Preacher, what is your greatest ambition in life?" Higgins responded, "To pilot men to the skies." The name stuck and from that point on, he and all the other traveling lumberjack preachers came to be known as the sky pilots of the North woods. In 1965, Rev. Frank Reed published *Lumberjack Sky Pilots,** a book describing the ministries of several of his fellow sky pilots. At the end of his own 48 year ministry he calculated that he had traveled over 75,000 miles on foot, and drove over 1,450,000 miles visiting logging camps. And he did it all out of his

desire to help pilot those men, as Paul put it, "heavenward" (Phil 3:14).

Clearly, Rev. Reed and his fellow sky pilots loved God. It is equally clear from Reed's writings, that they all had a special love and appreciation for his natural world. Reed once described a snowy trail, the reflection of a mountain lake, a mountain waterfall and wrote, "It is one of the spots where one feels the presence of the Great Creator who is the Author of all beauty and at the same time the Father of the individual." The lumberjack sky pilots spent their lives trekking through the woods for the sole purpose of sharing the love of God with those who would not, otherwise, have heard it. But once they heard, I am sure they, too, came to feel the presence of their Heavenly Father there in the midst of his magnificent creation.

* North Country Press, Utica, NY, 1965 and 2000

Nature Journal

82. The Operation

*Let us fix our eyes on Jesus, the author and perfecter
of our faith . . . (Heb. 12:2)*

The Trek:
Read Hebrews 12:1-13

Nature Reflections:
"The next 24 hours will be critical" the doctor announced.
My dad had just undergone heart surgery. When I finally got
home I went right to the dock to pray. Here at the water's
edge I often experienced God's peace. Tonight, however, a
bitter wind was blowing and the normally tranquil waters
were churning as tumultuously as the thoughts within me. I
looked into the sky and saw only darkness as a thick layer of
clouds completely enshrouded every speck of celestial light.
It certainly appeared I would find no peace here tonight. As
I stood there, deeply engrossed in thought, I became aware
of an increasing brightness over the water. I looked up and
saw the moon slowly emerging from behind a cloud. The
waves suddenly came alive as the moonlight danced across
the surface. The previously angry sounding waters sparkled
with animated exuberance. The darkness was broken by this
dazzling display of lights.

The message was clear. The peace I so desperately needed could only be found in looking to the true Light. Jesus knows my heart, sees my anguish, and cares even more about my dad than I do. We may not always understand why he allows us to go through the trials we face. We may not see any purpose behind our present pain, "But we see Jesus . . ." (Heb 2:9). I went back inside renewed and refreshed. I wouldn't know the outcome of dad's operation until tomorrow. But God's operation on my heart was a success. The darkness in my spirit was broken by his dazzling Light. My eyes were fixed, once again, on the One who holds our lives in his loving hands. Jesus would keep the light of his love shining for both me and my dad, tonight, tomorrow and forever.

Nature Journal

83. Defense Mechanisms

All kinds of animals, birds, reptiles and creatures of the sea are being tamed and have been tamed by man, but no man can tame the tongue. It is a restless evil, full of deadly poison.
(James 3:7,8)

The Trek:
Read James 3

Nature Reflections:

I got home just after sunset but still attempted to get in my jog before dark. As I came around the bend I nearly ran over a skunk contentedly minding his own business at the side of the road. I regrouped midair and just narrowly missed landing on him as I jogged on by. The skunk seemed oblivious to me, but my heart had skipped a beat as images of tomato soup baths danced before my eyes. Despite their malodorous reputation, skunks are actually one of the gentlest and least aggressive creatures in the woods. They will spray if they feel threatened, but skunks usually prefer not to, and will give plenty of warning before they do. But once sufficiently provoked, they can fire up to six rounds of their stinky oily fluid with lightening speed and great accuracy. While it smells like a lot more, each dose is actually only a fraction of a teaspoon.

165

Don't think too unkindly of these creatures, however. Skunks only spray as a defense mechanism that protects them from their predators.

We humans have a few defense mechanisms of our own, and we have been known to release them with far less provocation than needed by the skunk. If we feel attacked or insulted, we can respond with a battery of words far more destructive than a little skunk oil. No amount of tomato juice can repair the damages done by our spray of angry words. Nor are there any angry-word protection products on the market just yet. Just how important are our words to God? James writes, "If anyone considers himself religious and yet does not keep a tight rein on his tongue, he deceives himself and his religion is worthless" (James 1:26). You might say, hurtful words really stink!

Nature Journal

84. Metamorphosis

For you have been born again, not of perishable seed, but of imperishable, through the living and enduring word of God.
(1 Pet. 1:23)

The Trek:
Read 1 Peter 1:6-23

Nature Reflections:

As kids, we called them "wooly bears." We would pick them up and gently pet their bristly backs. As fun as they were to play with, the true wonder of caterpillars wasn't in what they were, but what we knew they would one day become. The sluggish little earthbound wooly bear would soon be transformed into a lovely butterfly that would gracefully soar through the skies. The process that turns the caterpillar into a butterfly is called metamorphosis which literally means "to change form." There are actually four stages the butterfly goes through to arrive at its graceful adult stage which includes the egg, the larva (caterpillar), pupa (cocoon) and finally, the adult butterfly.

In many ways, the transformation in the life of the Christian is similar to the four stages of the butterfly. The egg stage could be compared to one's physical birth. At birth, we enter the larva stage. We eat, we grow, and that just about summarizes our lives apart from God. We live to satisfy our own needs. The caterpillar must enter its cocoon if it is to move on to the next stage of life. As humans, we must make a similar choice if we are to leave this selfish life behind and enter a new one by faith. Once in its cocoon, the caterpillar merely goes to sleep while all those marvelous changes take place. Similarly, the changes in a believer's life don't happen because of any work on his part, but because of the work Jesus did on his behalf on the cross. The former unbeliever rises from his prayer of faith, born again. At that point it is only a matter of time until the metamorphosis is complete and the believer will start to soar upon his new wings of faith.

Nature Journal

85. Changed for Good

For, "All men are like grass, and all their glory is like the flowers of the field; the grass withers and the flowers fall, but the word of the Lord stands forever."
(1 Pet. 1:24, 25)

The Trek:
Read 1 Peter 1:24-25 and Isaiah 40:1-8

Nature Reflections:
The monarch butterfly landed gracefully on my new butterfly bush. Not long ago, this lovely creature had been crawling on the ground concerned only about what was for lunch. Now it was an airborne symbol of the wonder and assurance of our salvation. Imagine, for a moment, a butterfly who decided it didn't want to be a butterfly after all. What if it were to prefer life back on the ground? Now, that butterfly might attempt to go back to the old ways. It could hang out on the ground with the other caterpillars and refuse to fly. Yet, no matter how hard it tried, that butterfly could not become a caterpillar again. All it would accomplish was to give up all the benefits of being a butterfly choosing, instead, to go back to struggling along on the ground and become an easy prey for

its predators. But once the metamorphosis was complete the creature would always remain a butterfly.

Such is the case of a believer. When we ask Jesus into our hearts we are, in his own words, "born again." We have been permanently reborn into God's eternal family. We could, of course, choose not live as children of God. Like the prodigal son we could walk away from our Heavenly Father and spend our earthly lives in spiritual bankruptcy (which is as silly as a butterfly wanting to crawl). Yet, even then, we remain his children. Nothing can change the fact that we belong to him. What a joy and assurance to know that when we give our lives to Jesus it is forever. He has transformed us into new creatures, freed from our earthly bondage, and freed to soar into eternity with him. Like the butterfly we have truly been changed . . . for good.

Nature Journal

86. Tension Rocks

As you come to him, the living Stone—rejected by men but chosen by God and precious to him—you also, like living stones, are being built into a spiritual house.
(1 Pet. 2:4, 5)

The Trek:
Read 1 Peter 2

Nature Reflections:
We called them "tension rocks." A trip to Lake Ontario always meant a trip home with a bucket of rocks. Not just any rocks, but the smooth, round rocks found on its beaches. The rocks come in many colors and are a wide assortment of rock and mineral types. What they all have in common is their trip through the natural rock tumbling process of this ocean-like body of fresh water. Through years of being pounded by waves, their rough edges have been slowly chiseled away leaving them almost perfectly smooth and round. As kids, we would each choose a favorite rock and start carrying it around with us, often rubbing and working it with our hands. That's where the name, "tension rock" came from. Eventually, the natural oil from our hands gave the already smooth surface an almost polished looking shine.

God uses a finishing process on his children that one could compare to that of my tension rocks. First, he allows us to be placed into the natural tumbling process of life. Like the rocks in rough waters, the difficulties, pressures and hard times we face pound us until at times we feel as though we'll break into pieces. God actually uses those times in our lives more than any others to smooth our rough edges and strengthen our faith in him. But he doesn't stop there. He picks us up and carries us with him at all times. He continually holds us and we are further polished by his gentle hands. Now, when a rock is professionally shaped and polished it becomes a precious gem. Even before God began, we were precious to him, but once he has completed his work in our lives we'll have a "faith—of greater worth than gold" (1 Pet. 1:7).

Nature Journal

87. Seeking Whom He May Devour

Photo courtesy Jennifer Barnard

Your enemy the devil prowls around like a roaring lion looking for someone to devour.
(1 Pet. 5:8)

The Trek:
Read 1 Peter 5:1-11

Nature Reflections:
I've already mentioned our neighbor's cat Mike who freely roams the wild area out behind our house. More accurately, Mike freely *rules* the area. Every day, Mike can be seen patrolling his domain making certain that he and he alone reigns supreme. This gives us the added benefit of our own private garden police. As long as Mike is on duty, no bunny or woodchuck dares nibble a flower anywhere within his kingdom's borders. I mentioned how much we appreciated Mike's vigilance on our behalf to his owner one day. She laughed and said that giving their pet such freedom had its disadvantages. Mike was constantly returning home with such morsels as dead birds, mice, squirrels, and even once, a half a snake (one must pause to wonder where the other half ended up). For Mike, these were trophies of war. For his owner . . . well, they were dead animals.

When Mike deposits his spoils proudly at his owner's feet, he is doing exactly what he was created to do. Cats are predators by nature. They were designed to hunt and catch their prey and they are, naturally, very good at it. It is no wonder that the Bible uses one of Mike's cousins to illustrate Satan. He, too, is a predator and for a time this earth is his dominion. He is our most powerful and dangerous enemy. However, those who have entrusted their lives to God need not fear him. Why? Because God's children are no longer citizens of this world, nor are they controlled by its evil interim king. We have become citizens of God's kingdom. When Jesus returns to earth he will reclaim what is rightfully his and Satan will be rendered powerless against him. No wonder the Scriptures refer to Jesus as our Lion of Judah!

Nature Journal

88. Falling Ahead

*To him who is able to keep you from falling
and to present you before his glorious
presence without fault and with great joy.*
(Jude 1:24)

The Trek:

Read Jude 1:17-25

Nature Reflections:

We have always had finches at the bird feeder outside our bedroom window. Once we put out the special finch feeder full of black thistle, however, the numbers quadrupled. The sociable little goldfinches, in particular, appeared in such numbers and with such commotion that I stopped using an alarm clock in the morning. Instead, I merely started getting up with the finches. As their name indicates, goldfinches are easily identified by their bright yellow color. They are easily attracted by thistle and are fairly unafraid of humans watching them from close by. One of the most fascinating features of these little birds is their unique method of flight. We watch with delight as they flit in and away from the feeder. The flight of the goldfinch is performed in deep curved lines alternatively rising and falling after each propelling motion of its wings. With each rise and fall, the finch will commonly utter a two or three note song while ascending.

The goldfinch's pattern of rising and falling beautifully portrays the earthly walk of the believer. We all understand that this life is an ongoing set of ups and downs, highs and lows, successes and failures. We were even forewarned in the Scriptures that "In this world you will have trouble . . ." (John 16:33). We were never promised smooth sailing or a straight, upward flight. What we were promised was Jesus' response to our tribulations: ". . . But take heart! I have overcome the world." So, next time you find yourself in one of those downward spins, picture the little goldfinch in flight and rest in the promise that "The LORD upholds all those who fall and lifts up all who are bowed down" (Ps. 145:14). Then you can utter a little song of joy knowing you, too, will soon be ascending.

Nature Journal

89. Full Circle

At once I was in the Spirit, and there before me was a throne in heaven with someone sitting on it. And the one who sat there had the appearance of jasper and carnelian. A rainbow, resembling an emerald, encircled the throne.
(Rev. 4:2, 3)

The Trek:
Read Revelation 4

Nature Reflections:
When I spotted the magnificent rainbow arcing over the lake from one horizon to the other, I ran and got the camcorder to capture it on film. Later that evening, Bob enjoyed the show but was especially impressed with the sound effects I had unwittingly recorded as I oohed and ahhhed as the camera was rolling. Though it is sometimes described as having seven colors, the rainbow is actually a continuum of colors from red to violet. The red outer band makes an angle of 42° with the sun; the other colors making successively smaller angles. Since the rainbow can only be seen between 40-42° we do not see the full circle of a rainbow because the earth gets in the way. The lower the sun is to the horizon the more of the circle we see so at sunset we have the best chance of

seeing a full semicircle. However, if the observer is located in a high enough place, such as an airplane, one could conceivably see a complete circular rainbow.

While most of us will not see one in our lifetime, some of us will have the opportunity to see a full rainbow in the future. The Bible speaks of a rainbow completely encircling the Lord's heavenly throne. Remember, God first gave the rainbow as a promise to Noah. However, Noah really only saw a half-rainbow. Like the rainbow, God has given us many other promises that, at this point, we only see in part. As Paul put it, "Now I know in part; then I shall know fully, even as I am fully known" (1 Cor. 13:12). We don't see it all at this time but we've been shown enough to know that if we wait out the storm, the best is yet to come.

Nature Journal

90. The Grand Finale

The Spirit and the bride say, "Come!" And let him who hears say, "Come!" Whoever is thirsty, let him come; and whoever wishes, let him take the free gift of the water of life.
(Rev. 22:17)

The Trek:
Read Revelation 22

Nature Reflections:
It was our last day at camp for the season and we were using every possible excuse to linger as long as we could before having to make that final trip home. Just one more ship had to go by, one last peanut to our favorite chipmunk. And of course, one last sunset. Once the sun had fallen below the horizon it appeared that our excuses had run out. We began to move begrudgingly toward the car when I heard that beloved sound in the distance. "A loon," I whispered, but Bob was already heading back to the dock. Sure enough, we saw the lone bird slowly making its way down the River toward us. With the backdrop of a spectacular post-sunset glow, Bob ran the video camera as I sat in silent awe. It was the perfect end to summer.

The magic of those last moments at camp communicated God's love to me on a very personal level. Yes, God does know how to do great finales. But, as the saying goes, "You ain't seen nothing yet!" The short season of life on this planet is nearing an end. Maybe in our lifetime; maybe not. Either way, whenever it takes place, God has a Grand Finale planned that will surpass anything we have ever seen, heard, or could imagine. To some, the end of the world is a fearful thought. But it needn't be because, as God himself, put it he is "not wanting anyone to perish, but everyone to come to repentance" (2 Pet. 3:9). Everyone has been invited to drink of the Water of Life. And all who do will discover that just after the last sunset here on earth, we'll make that final trip Home to our new waterfront property on his River of Life.

Nature Journal

Made in the USA
Charleston, SC
16 October 2013